PRAISE FOR *A Place Called Blessing*

"I love a great story—especially one that captures both my mind and my spirit. In *A Place Called Blessing* we get both: a compelling story and a deep understanding of the essential need for every person to receive the gift of unconditional love and acceptance from their parents. How do you give this blessing? Turn the page and read for yourself."

— GARY SMALLEY
Author, *Guarding Your Child's Heart*

"If you have children in your life, then give them and yourself a gift by reading *A Place Called Blessing*. You'll be stirred, encouraged, and forever changed by this deeper understanding of God's intention for parents to bless their children."

— ANDY ANDREWS
New York Times best-selling author,
The Noticer and *The Traveler's Gift*

"If you've ever doubted your ability to be a vessel of grace and healing in the life of someone who's hurting, you need to read *A Place Called Blessing*. It is the story of a wounded soul named Josh, but chances are there is a Josh living next door to you or even sitting near you in the pew at church."

— JIM DALY
President, Focus on the Family

"Redemption! We all long for it. Some fear they may never find it. In this masterfully crafted story, John Trent reminds us that no one is beyond the reach of love's redeeming power. No matter how far or difficult the journey, there is a place called *blessing* for each of us!"

— DAVID LIVINGSTONE
HENDERSON, MD
Coauthor, *Finding Purpose Beyond
Our Pain*; Hope for the Heart Chair of
Counseling and Psychology, Criswell
College; adjunct professor, Dallas
Theological Seminary

"Happy endings aren't just for fairy tales—they can be the stuff of life if God is given the opportunity to redeem the circumstances and individuals involved. *A Place Called Blessing* is that kind of story, proving that endings, while not always perfect, can truly be happy and blessed."

— CLAUDIA AND DAVID ARP, MSW
Authors, 10 Great Dates series

"When God gives a writer a life message, it is inscribed upon his heart and spirit. It's not that other great books don't come out of the author, but you always remember their finest work. John Trent's *The Blessing* is John's life message. And now in novel form *A Place Called Blessing* will reach down into your own spirit and heart and bless you beyond measure."

— DR. GARY and BARB ROSBERG
America's Family Coaches; coauthors,
6 Secrets to a Lasting Love

A PLACE CALLED
BLESSING

Books Authored or Coauthored by John Trent

The Blessing
The Two Sides of Love
The Language of Love
LifeMapping
Love for All Seasons
The Light of Home
Dad's Everything Book for Daughters
Go the Distance
Choosing to Live the Blessing
Faith Launch
My Mother's Hands
Chasing Skinny Rabbits
The Gift of Honor
HeartShift
The 2-Degree Difference
Love Is a Decision

CHILDREN'S BOOKS

I'd Choose You!
The Treasure Tree
The Two Trails
There's a Duck in My Closet!
Spider Sisters
Superhero Swamp

A PLACE CALLED
BLESSING

Where Hurting Ends and Love Begins

John Trent, PhD
with Annette Smith

THOMAS NELSON
Since 1798

NASHVILLE   DALLAS   MEXICO CITY   RIO DE JANEIRO

Published in Nashville, Tennessee, by Thomas Nelson. Thomas Nelson is a registered trademark of Thomas Nelson, Inc.

Published in association with the literary agency of Alive Communications, Inc., 7680 Goddard Street, Suite 200, Colorado Springs, CO 80920. www.alivecommunications.com.

Thomas Nelson, Inc., titles may be purchased in bulk for educational, business, fund-raising, or sales promotional use. For information, please e-mail SpecialMarkets@ThomasNelson.com.

Library of Congress Cataloging-in-Publication Data

Trent, John, 1952–
    A place called Blessing : where hurting ends and love begins / John Trent with Annette Smith.
    p. cm.
    ISBN 978-0-8499-4618-9 (pbk.)
    1. Blessing and cursing. 2. Parenting—Religious aspects— Christianity. 3. Self-esteem—Religious aspects—Christianity. I. Smith, Annette Gail, 1959– II. Title. III. Title: Where hurting ends and love begins.
    BV4509.5.T696 2011
    231'.5—dc22   2010050657

Printed in the United States of America

11 12 13 14 15 RRD 5 4 3 2 1

To Dr. Ted and Lynn Kitchens

Years ago, my wife, Cindy, and I were struggling to start a new seminar ministry with a new message based on a new book called *The Blessing.*

The first church in the country to take the risk and host my seminar was Christ Chapel in Fort Worth, Texas, pastored by Dr. Ted and Lynn Kitchens.

Ted and Lynn's love, counsel, and encouragement continue to be incredible blessings to Cindy and me.

And the thousands of people who attend Christ Chapel today know what Cindy and I know. When you walk into Ted and Lynn's home or visit their women's ministry or show up at their church, you truly have found "a place called Blessing."

Acknowledgments

HEARTFELT THANKS AND boundless admiration go out to Annette Smith. Her ability to come alongside me and aid in capturing the deep emotions invoked when hurting people gain or miss the blessing is a God-given gift.

And there would be no *A Place Called Blessing* had not Debbie Wickwire at Thomas Nelson listened with her heart and acted boldly. She became the champion at Nelson for relaunching the timeless message of the blessing in this new form for a new generation of readers.

Cindy and I are deeply appreciative to you both.

We believe every reader will be as well.

Introduction

A PLACE CALLED BLESSING is a dream come true for me. For years I have shared the message of the biblical blessing with men and women across the country and across the world. Yet here, finally, is a way to communicate this life-changing message in a new way for a new generation of readers—not by sharing studies and overhead points and sidebars, but in story form. By portraying human interactions in such a compelling way that the reality of God's blessing comes alive for readers and becomes a part of their own real-life stories.

A Place Called Blessing paints a vivid picture of what it means to choose blessings over curses, light over darkness, life over death. It is the story of one young man's struggle to believe he could ever be worthy of *anyone's* blessing and one young woman's longing to be loved and affirmed despite the fear that it will never happen for her. More important, it shows what happens when a hurting family chooses to live the blessing. I hope it points the way toward a real place called Blessing in your life. Believe me, it is the kind of place you will want to find and share with those you love.

So it is with great joy that I sign off for now and invite you to sit back, turn the page, and step into the story of a young boy named Josh. I will join you again at the end of the book.

— JOHN TRENT, PHD
President, StrongFamilies.com
and *The Institute for the*
Blessing at Barclay College

 One

MOST EVERY KID has a special toy or blanket he likes to have with him at bedtime or when he is scared or upset. You know, something to hold that helps him go to sleep and makes him feel safe. You probably had one. Or your kids did. Maybe for you it was a teddy bear, a pillow, or a blanket—a gift from your mom or your dad, maybe your grandma. Mine was a tan rabbit with soft fur and silky ears that I rubbed between my fingers as I fell asleep.

But I didn't get that rabbit from my parents or my grand-parents. Nope. Not that rabbit or any other toy. I never met my grandparents, and my parents were really young when they had me and my two brothers, Sam and Matt. Young and dumb, as they say.

My dad did not go to work very often. My mom wasn't big on cooking or cleaning or taking care of kids. What they liked to do was go out with their friends. Every weekend and lots of weeknights, the two of them went out drinking and partying. Every time they went, they would promise to bring us boys a treat or a toy if we were good.

I think we were good. Maybe not. All I know is most of

the time they forgot. We rarely got treats, and we didn't have many toys.

Once when I was pretty little, Mom and Dad took me and my brothers with them. They stopped on the way at a gas station and got us Honey Buns. Our mom gave us a blanket that was in the front seat. When we got to the bar, they left us in the car. It was only supposed to be a little while, but I guess they forgot. Matt and Sam and I fell asleep and did not wake up until the cops came and opened up the doors. Somebody had seen us and called. The cops did not have to break a window or anything because my dad had not locked the doors. They just pulled us out and put us in the back of their car, then went inside to get our parents. When they found them, they put them in a different cop car.

That's when I got the rabbit. In our state, lots of communities have this program called Caring Cops. It has been around for a long time. The way it works is, police officers carry stuffed animals in their trunks to give to kids who might be scared or upset. All three of us got one.

If you ask me, whoever came up with that had a good idea.

That night they put my parents in jail, and we boys went to this place where they had lots of beds for kids. They gave us some food and some clean clothes. We only stayed there one night. Before our parents could take us home, they had to promise not to make that mistake again.

Sure enough, they learned their lesson. From then on, they left us at home when they went out. I was four, almost five. Matt was six, and Sam was seven.

I do not remember my parents hitting us or spanking us. They yelled sometimes, but mostly at each other. I guess we did not cause them too much trouble because they pretty much ignored us. We were sort of like the furniture. Just . . . there. They did not touch us or talk to us much. They slept till noon usually, leaving us to fend for ourselves.

We looked out for one another, as best as little kids could. We played with stuff like cans and boxes. We had sword fights with wire coat hangers. I'm surprised nobody's eye got put out. Sometimes we wrestled. Most days we ate cereal from the box and drank orange soda. Our couch had three cushions, one each for my brothers and me to sleep on. Every night we pulled them off the couch and lined them up in a row against the wall. My parents slept on a mattress on the floor.

We didn't go outside. We didn't go to school. But we did watch TV.

It was on 24/7.

Early one Sunday morning, I guess my dad must have gotten confused driving home from a bar. No one ever did tell us the whole story. I heard a cop saying later that he was glad no one else was killed. Of course, at the time I did not understand what he meant.

I am not sure how they found out about us, but when the police came to our apartment after the accident, they found me and my brothers asleep on our couch cushions. We woke up confused and afraid, but we didn't cry. We had learned early on that crying didn't exactly do us any good.

"Where's our mom?" my oldest brother, Sam, asked one of the cops standing at the door.

He looked over at his partner. "Uh, she had to go somewhere."

"How about our dad?"

"He went with her."

"So they're coming home soon?" I remember asking.

They looked at each other again as if they did not know.

"Hey, I bet you boys are hungry," the first cop said. "Let's go get you something to eat."

We weren't sure about leaving. Mom and Dad had told us to stay put. But these guys were police officers, and from our experience they were people who had been nice to us. You could trust them. Besides, we *were* hungry.

"Come on, fellows," said the cop. "It'll be all right."

We didn't exactly have a choice, so we went. None of us had on pajamas. We did not own any. We slept in the same clothes we wore all day, which were the same clothes we wore most days. None of us wore underwear. We had finished off the cereal earlier in the day, so there was no food in the house. The apartment was dark. Even the TV was black because our electricity had been turned off the day before.

It was getting light by the time we got to the police station. We sat side by side on a sticky plastic couch while they called for a social worker to come and get us. Our hair was long. It had been more than two weeks since any of us had taken a bath. The officers had driven us by McDonald's to get breakfast. Biscuits with sausage inside. We ate them without saying a word.

Every time a new person came to check on us, we asked him about our mom and our dad. Again and again, the cops told us the same thing.

"Don't worry."

"Everything's going to be all right."

WE HAD BEEN at the police station for two hours before the social worker finally showed up. She took us to a room without any windows, and one of the cops went with her. He stood in the corner. She sat down at a little table. We had to sit down, too, but there were not enough chairs, and I had to sit in my oldest brother's lap.

"When do we get to see our parents?" he asked.

"I'm sorry, but you're not going to be able to see them again." She held a wad of Kleenex in her hand. "There was a wreck. On the highway. Your parents died in an accident."

We started crying then, all of us at once. The social worker tried to hug us, but I pulled away. I was mad.

Everyone had been telling us everything would be all right. But this was not right! I ran over to the cop and started hitting and kicking him.

Our parents were not much, but they were all we had.

MOST PEOPLE HAVE some kind of family ties. Relatives, even if they live far away, who will help out when there is a real need. The social workers tried and tried to find somebody like that who would take in my brothers and me, but they had no such luck.

Nobody wanted us.

Which was how we ended up in foster care.

Like most, our state is pretty short of foster homes. Some counties don't have a single home. At any given time, it can be a challenge for a social worker to place one kid. Finding a home to take three brothers on short notice was an impossible task. So we were separated for the first time ever in our lives.

When my brothers got into a car to be taken away, I tried to run after them, but a big man grabbed me. He picked me up and held me tight. I cried and fought against him, trying to get down. Why were they going and not me? What had I done bad?

You can listen to the news and know that the foster-care

system has a lot of problems. But I have to give them credit for one thing. They tried to make it where my brothers and I got to see each other on a regular basis. The plan was for us to get together once a month. That may sound like a lot, but to a little kid a month is the same thing as a year. And sometimes it worked out, but sometimes it did not. Or two of us would make it, but the other one would not.

I UNDERSTAND IT better now. People are busy, especially people who take care of lots of kids. Things happen. But I didn't understand it then. All I knew was they would tell me I was going to see my brothers, and then it didn't happen. It just started eating at me. A lot of things did.

Not many kids get to stay in the same foster home for very long. I lost count of how many different ones I got sent to. Some places I would go to for just one night while they tried to find someplace else for me to go. Others lasted longer—weeks or months, maybe. I was still pretty little then, so my sense of time passing was not all that good.

One foster mom told me she was thinking about adopting me. She was going to see if she could get my brothers too. I was so excited. Finally, a real family for me. I couldn't stop thinking about how great everything was going to be. I hoped it would happen soon. But a few days later I came in from playing and saw that Foster Mom was packing up my stuff. No way. I started crying and asked her why she was doing that. Had she been lying to me all along? I got mad and pulled all the books and toys off the shelf in my room. I threw those books and toys as far and as hard as I could.

Foster Mom would not look at me. She did not even yell at me for throwing stuff. She just kept on putting my stuff into a big plastic bag. There were problems, and she had changed her mind. She was sorry, but my social worker was on her way to get me to take me somewhere else.

When stuff like that happens to you as a kid, you eventually learn to expect most everything to go bad. You just kind of give up. That's what I did, anyway. I stopped counting on things and believing people. I didn't ever feel safe, couldn't ever let my guard down. Think about it. I had been shown that even if people say they care about you and they want you, they can change their minds.

It is easy to say I stopped trusting when I went to foster care, but that is not when it started. No, it was way before that. When your parents don't come when you cry, don't feed you when you're hungry, don't pick you up when you fall, you learn that you can't count on anyone.

But then something unexpected happened. I was six years old when my foster mom at the time told me I was leaving her house to go to a new home. She packed my clothes into a bag, my tan rabbit too. I wasn't surprised that I had to leave. The day before I had hit her real son when he told me I was stupid. Before that, I had wet the bed three nights in a row.

But this time I wasn't leaving because of fighting or doing anything else wrong. I did not know it at the time, but I was about to experience one of the best days of my life.

Or the worst, depending on how you look at it.

 # Two

WHEN THE SOCIAL worker came to pick me up, she told me she had a surprise. I ran to the car, hoping it was some candy or gum, but it turned out to be way better than that. When I got almost to the car, two heads popped up from where they had been hiding, ducked down in the backseat. My brothers were laughing their heads off. I learned that they were going to the new home too. We would all be in the same foster home at the same time.

My brothers and I hugged and poked one another and tickled and laughed while the social worker drove. Looking back, I realize I did not care what the house looked like or even if the other kids there were big and mean. I was so glad to be with my brothers, nothing else mattered in the whole world.

Since I was the last one in, I had a seat by the window. We drove and drove, from one end of town to the other, faster and farther, to where there weren't many houses. Just lots of trees and fences and even cows and some horses.

"Are we almost there?" I needed to use the bathroom.

"How much farther?" asked Sam.

"Is there a mom and a dad?" asked Matt. His last home

was with a lady who did not have a husband. He was the only boy in a family with three girls. His room was pink.

She smiled at us in the mirror. The job of a social worker cannot be easy. She was probably smiling because her task of transporting three rowdy brothers was almost to its end. But we never knew.

"Start watching, guys." She slowed the car and turned down a little road. Trees grew so close they touched overhead; it felt as though we were going through a tunnel. Like always when I was about to see a new home, my stomach got jerky. I put my hand to my mouth and chewed on the knuckle of my left thumb.

Pretty soon, we drove out of the tree tunnel and started up a driveway. We boys stopped talking. We had been through this so many times before. Would the family be nice? Would they let us watch TV? Would we get food that we liked? Would there be lots of kids, or would we be the only ones?

The driveway was bumpy. Even though the car wasn't stopped and we knew better, we unlatched our seat belts so we could see better. There weren't any other houses around. This one was white with black shutters and a red front door. Old. Pretty big. And with a porch on the front. There was a big wooden garage off to one side, separate from the house. The yard had a swing set and a sandbox and tall yellow flowers growing on each side of the sidewalk that led up to the front steps.

"Get your bags, boys." The social worker opened up the trunk. Then she led the way up the sidewalk. We climbed the wide wooden steps and took a look around the porch. There was a swing and a couple of chairs, some plants, a watering can, and a little brown dog. I tried to pet him, but he jumped off the porch and ran around to the back of the house.

Before she even knocked, our new foster mom opened the door. She was young and pretty. And black . . . which my brothers and I were not. We looked at one another. This was something the social worker had forgotten to tell us. But I guess she had remembered to tell Foster Mom because she did not seem surprised at all.

She told us to come on in. Foster Dad would be home in a couple of hours. He was out on the tractor, cutting hay. No, she didn't have any kids. Just us. But she had been taking care of foster kids for ten years. She wasn't as young as she looked.

Foster Mom showed us around downstairs—the kitchen; the living room, where there was a TV; and the room where she and Foster Dad slept. Then we climbed the stairs to what she called *the attic*. Two rooms. The ceiling sloped on the sides, and there was a big window in the end.

One of the rooms had three beds. I was glad to see that. I couldn't wait to sleep next to my brothers again. The other room had toys and books, an art easel and paints, and a CD player with a bunch of music she said we could play whenever we wanted. There wasn't a bathroom, so we would have to go downstairs for that, but we didn't care. She showed us where we were supposed to put our clothes; then she and the social worker went downstairs so they could fill out the papers.

We sat down, each of us on our beds. We had been through this before. Meet Foster Mom. See your room. Put your stuff away. Meet Foster Dad later—if there was a dad. My older brothers agreed this was a pretty good place. I wanted to go look for that dog.

"Boys, come downstairs, please." It was the social worker. She told us she was leaving, but she would come back to check on us in a week. Then she left.

"You boys hungry?"

The first thing new foster moms always ask after the social worker leaves is if you want a snack. A kid always does. We had peanut butter on crackers and then some apple slices.

As I sat at the table in the kitchen, my feet didn't reach the floor. "Where's your dog?" I asked.

"Toby? You want to see him?" Foster Mom opened the back door and called. In a minute he ran in and started sniffing my feet. Foster Mom gave me a cup with some dog food in it. "You want to give him his dinner? His bowl is right there." She pointed.

I slid out of the chair and took the cup of food from her. Toby wagged his tail. When I poured the food into his bowl, he ate it all really fast. I knelt down to pet him. When he licked my hand, it tickled. I scratched his chin. He rolled over for me to rub his belly.

"YOU GUYS CAN look around outside." Foster Mom saw we had finished our snacks. "Go anywhere you want in the yard. There's swings and a creek around back. Some of the neighbor kids might be playing down there. Just stay inside the fence and on this side of the creek. You've got on sneakers, don't you?" She looked at our feet. "Good. If you get muddy, we'll just put them in the wash."

She walked with us toward the door. "You ever seen a real creek?"

"Sure," my oldest brother said. "I stayed in a house with one right behind us. They're cool."

We headed the way Foster Mom pointed.

I had never lived in the country, not even with any of my foster parents. When you looked past the trees at the edge of the yard, you could see there were other houses, but not close.

Cows grazed on the other side of the fence, goats climbed up on a pile of boulders, and a bunch of chickens pecked at the ground near the swing set. I picked up a stick and whacked at a patch of tall grass.

A trail sloped downhill from the edge of the yard. Below, a trickle of water flowed between two sandy, sloping banks. Nothing like a river. Not any deeper than the tops of our ankles. But something to see just the same.

We crouched at the side of the creek and watched tiny gray fish swim past. My oldest brother stood up and walked a ways upstream. Sam and I stayed behind, watching the fish.

"Hey," he called. "It's wider down here. And I think I found a turtle."

We scampered down to where he was. Sure enough, it was a turtle. One of my foster families had one that stayed in a big glass cage with a little plastic tree inside. That turtle was little. This one was as big as my shoe.

"Don't touch him," said Matt. "He might bite." He tossed some dirt clods at the turtle, which made him pull his head into his shell.

"You scared him."

But then the turtle put his head back out. He wasn't scared for long. We stood there watching as he crawled toward the bank, then slid in and swam away.

"Hey."

We jumped at the sound of somebody behind us. Two kids, a boy and a girl, walked toward us. He had red hair. Hers was light blonde.

"You the new foster kids?" The boy was barefoot, and his jeans were cut off at the knee.

We didn't answer, just looked at our feet. Being a foster kid was not something you went around telling people.

"Our house is back there." He pointed at a brown house a ways beyond the creek.

"We're sister and brother." The girl looked about the same age as me. "Are there any girls?"

"No." I was the first one to speak. "Just us."

"I wish you had girls." She bent down to pick up a pretty rock.

"Wanna play?" asked the boy.

Sam nodded. "Sure."

And so we did. That day and almost every day after that. Kids make friends so much more easily than adults. It was the third day before we even knew each other's names.

Since it was summer there wasn't any school except Sunday school. Foster Mom and Dad took us there every Sunday morning. But every weekday morning we would eat breakfast, brush our teeth, and make our beds, then race out the door to meet our friends. We waded in the creek and built bridges, booby traps, and a fort, all out of fallen-down branches and other stuff we found in the woods near the edge of the water.

At noon, Foster Mom would blow a whistle, and we would come in for lunch. Usually it was sandwiches, milk, and chips at a picnic table just outside the back kitchen door. Sometimes our friends ate with us. Foster Mom was friends with their mom, and she would call and make sure it was okay.

We never went to their house to eat or play. I remember asking Foster Mom why. She told me it was because we were foster kids and she felt better with us being where she could keep a close eye on us.

We kids squeezed every possible minute of playtime out of those long summer days. Not until it was too dark to see would we reluctantly tell our friends good-bye. Then we would eat dinner with Foster Mom and Dad, take our baths, and go up to our room, where we would crawl into bed and talk until, one by one, we fell asleep.

Lying in my bed in that attic room, listening to the sounds of my brothers' breathing as they slept, I was content. And why not? My stomach was full. My clothes and my body were clean. Knowing Foster Mom and Dad were downstairs made me feel safe. Not once had they left us alone to fend for ourselves.

Did I trust them? Probably not 100 percent. I had learned that adults could go back on their word. They could lie to you and not even care. And they could die and leave you alone. But this foster mom and dad did seem better than the others. And being with my brothers helped more than I can describe.

My bed was against the wall with a window, and most nights I would push back the curtain and look out at the sky. Out there in the country, where there weren't many lights, you cannot imagine how beautiful and bright the stars were. I had never seen anything like them in any of my other homes. I would stare and stare at those stars until I would finally get sleepy. Then I would scoot down under the soft covers and close my eyes until morning.

 # Three

WHENEVER OUR FRIENDS got to stay for lunch, we would hang out on the front porch for a while after we ate, instead of going back down to the creek. Foster Mom usually liked for us to stay outside. I don't blame her. We were dirty as pigs by ten o'clock in the morning. But sometimes we would wash our hands, and she would hose us off from the knees down, and we would get to play inside. She had a bunch of games that she kept in a closet upstairs. Sam and Matt liked Monopoly. They said checkers was boring, but the girl and I sat and played game after game. At first she beat me over and over again, but it didn't take me long to get almost as good as her.

Because we were the youngest, there were days the three older boys would hang out and the girl and I would play together. We really didn't mind that they would leave us behind because we had a secret place to play that they did not know about—a hideout under the wooden front porch.

The house had no basement and did not sit on a concrete foundation. It was built up off the ground, supported by wooden piers and beams, with a crawl space under the entire house. To get into the space under the porch, you had to scoot on your belly through scratchy bushes. Once inside the space was sloped, and it was only in the tallest spot, under the top step, that we could sit up without bumping our heads.

Toby the dog liked it under the porch too. I do not know how he knew where we were, but every time we would sneak into our secret place, before long we would see him crashing through the bushes to join us.

The dirt felt cool and damp under our bare legs and feet. We built little hills and valleys and made roads that curved between them. The girl brought over a set of little plastic dolls. I would have been embarrassed for my brothers to see me playing dolls, but they weren't there to tease me, so it was fun. We pretended they were a family and built little houses for the dolls out of sticks and leaves.

The girl and I decorated our secret place with an assortment of toys and trinkets. Almost every time we played under the porch, we added to our hidden stash. I contributed a couple of old matchbox cars I had found in the back of the attic closet. She brought a mesh bag of seashells from her bottom dresser drawer. We were always on the lookout for bird feathers and pretty rocks. We lined our treasures up in rows on one side of our play space.

On cloudy days it was almost too dark to see underneath the porch. Only small slivers of light shone through the gaps between the overhead boards. Some days we would go under there but not stay because it was too dark to be fun. I asked Foster Mom if I could borrow a flashlight, but she said no.

One day the girl came up with a great idea. When her mother was in the other room, she opened a kitchen drawer and grabbed a candle and a box of matches, which she brought over the next day. We propped the candle in the dirt.

Neither of us had experience with matches, so it took several tries before we were able to strike one, and then a few more tries before we were able to light the candle. But when we succeeded, the flickering shadows it made transformed our play space into a mysterious, magical place. More daring, we held the candle above our heads to better see the boards above us. Braver still, we took turns holding it under our chins and making pretend scary faces at each other.

Once we knew how to light the candle, our hideaway became our favorite place to play. When our brothers would come looking for us, we would hear their footsteps over our heads and clamp our hands over our mouths to keep from laughing out loud. They would call and call, but we stayed right where we were, still and quiet as sneaky little mice.

Later, when they had given up looking, we would crawl our way out and head down to the creek. When they asked where we had been, we would just shrug. We would never tell.

WHEN YOU THINK about it, there was nothing that special about our foster home in the country. Foster Mom and Dad were not rich. They fed us, saw that we kept clean, and made sure we had decent clothes. They weren't exceptional parents. They were just normal.

But that summer, my brothers and I enjoyed as much happiness as we had ever experienced. From our point of view, we had it all—adults who treated us nice, friends to play with, and the barefoot freedom of living in the country. We didn't talk about it—maybe we were afraid it would be bad luck. But I hoped with everything in me that we would get to stay in this foster home forever. I'm sure my brothers hoped for the same thing.

Whenever I had to go to a new home, for the first few days I would be scared and keep quiet and stay on my best behavior, trying hard not to do anything wrong. Of course, that never lasted. So the longer we lived with these parents, the more relaxed I got. I lost some of the fear of being separated from my brothers and having to leave. I felt more at home and talked more to Foster Mom and Dad. I laughed when we were at the table and sometimes acted silly. I dared to disagree with things they told me, and a few times I even talked back. But because they were so kind and so fair, I did not much mind going to the time-out chair or getting a talking-to from Foster Dad.

I won't say I felt loved. But I did feel safe.

At least for a little while.

Until the bad thing happened.

It was a late August day. School was starting in a week, and I would be going to first grade. Foster Mom took us shopping for school supplies, new socks, shoes, and underwear. My brothers and I each had three new sets of school clothes.

We were excited about our new things but nervous about a new school. The social worker had helped Foster Mom fill out all the papers so we could go to the same school as our summertime friends. She had told us we would ride a big yellow bus that stopped at the end of the drive.

When the girl and her brother came over that day, we all spent the morning playing in the woods on the bank of the creek. When it got to be lunchtime, our friends went home but said they would be back. I wanted to show the girl my new school supplies. Her mother had not bought hers yet.

After we had eaten our sandwiches and chips, my brothers went back to the creek, but I stayed behind. I sat on the porch and tried to coax Toby into my lap. When he wouldn't come, I decided to crawl under the porch to my secret place. I would stay there until the girl came back.

Like most little boys I loved playing with cars. I drove them up and down roads I built in the dirt. Then I took the little dolls out of their blankets and pretended to give them rides. The last time we played, the little girl made houses out of sticks and dry leaves for each of them. After their ride I put them each in their houses.

It was not as much fun to play alone. I remember hoping my friend would be back soon. I played with a new feather we had found a few days before, and I rearranged the rock collection. Finally, I got around to messing with the candle.

We kept the matches in a plastic bag so they would stay dry. We had learned the hard way that when matches got wet, they were hard to start. We still had the first box that wouldn't strike, but now we had another one that would.

I set the candle in the sand then lit it. I wondered how that little bit of fire could make so much light. I loved to watch the flame flicker and jump. To a kid, especially a boy, fire is power and magic.

I had seen older kids at one of my other foster homes pass their fingers through the flame of a candle, so even though I was a little scared, I tried it. Surprise! It didn't burn. I tried it again. Still no burn. I decided maybe this was a special candle that wouldn't burn things.

I picked up one of the dolls. Would it burn? I passed it through the flame. No, it got warm, but it didn't burn. So I tried another doll. The other doll had been naked, but this one wore clothes. I didn't even pass her through the flame. When I put her close, her dress burst into flames.

Quickly I dropped the doll. She landed on her house of sticks and leaves. It, too, flamed up. I was scared, but I knew if you blew on a candle, it would make it go out, so I blew on the burning pile of sticks. It only made the flames rise higher.

Within seconds the other dolls' houses were on fire, too, and the secret place was filling up with smoke. I started coughing and choking.

I scrambled out through the bushes as quickly as I could, gulping air. Looking back, I could see the red glow of the fire under the porch. It was getting bigger.

What to do? Even though we had never talked about it, I knew better than to play with matches and fire. Foster Mom would be so mad, and I was going to be in so much trouble. I ran away from the house and hid in the garage, hoping the fire would go out by itself.

But it didn't.

I know now that flames spread along the wood supports, moving silently from the front to the rear, widening their path until the entire underside of the house was smoldering.

From my hiding place in the garage, I watched Foster Mom run from the back door of the house, then around the entire perimeter, looking for the fire. I heard her yell when she saw smoke billowing out from under the porch. She ran back inside. I'm guessing that's when she called the fire department. When she came back out, she picked up the garden hose, turned it on, then threw it down and began screaming for my brothers and me.

Pretty soon, two fire trucks and a sheriff's car pulled up into the yard. There weren't any fire hydrants close by, but one of the trucks had a big metal tank on it. Two firefighters pulled on a long brown hose, turned some dials and stuff, and began spraying water onto the roof.

Foster Dad came next. He was driving so fast I wasn't sure

he would stop. Neighborhood farmers pulled up behind him. I could hear everyone yelling and talking at once.

"I saw the smoke," Foster Dad said. "What happened?"

Foster Mom was crying. "I don't know. I was in the kitchen, and I thought I smelled something; then I went down the hall, and I saw smoke coming out the floor vents. I don't know. I don't know." Her hands covered her face.

"Is anyone inside?" the firefighters asked.

"No," Foster Mom told them. "The boys went outside after lunch." She pointed. "They're playing down at the creek."

Just then, Sam and Matt came racing toward the house.

"What's going on?" asked Sam.

The two of them looked all around, at the fire truck and the crowd of cars and at the house billowing smoke from underneath and now from above. I knew they were scared.

But not as scared as me.

"Where's your brother?" Foster Dad asked.

"I don't know."

"We haven't seen him since lunch."

"Who's missing?" asked a firefighter.

"Our other foster child. A little boy, six years old."

"And you don't know where he is?"

"He could be inside." One of the firefighters moved toward the house. Another turned to follow him.

"Oh God. Please. No," I heard Foster Mom say.

Both my brothers started to cry.

And the firefighters headed in.

Four

I SHOULD HAVE come out from the garage. I know I should have. But it was like I was frozen in place. Like my feet had gone dead beneath me. I couldn't move, and I couldn't speak.

When the firefighters went in, they risked their lives to find me. To save me. To rescue me.

But there was no rescue.

And no save.

Instead there was tragedy.

Grief.

And lives that were forever changed.

What the firefighters found when they went in that house was not me, but the girl. My friend. No one knew she was in the house. Everyone was left to guess what she had been doing inside, how long she had been there, or how she had gotten in without Foster Mom hearing her.

She was upstairs when they found her, lying on the floor in my room. Lifeless. Not breathing.

Someone jumped in their car to go get her parents. When the fireman came running down the steps of the house, carrying her, she looked like a big doll. I remember thinking maybe she was pretending to be asleep. We were always playing pretend. I couldn't believe there was anything really wrong with her.

But then the fireman laid her on the grass and tried to breathe into my friend's mouth. Over and over and over again, he leaned down and put his mouth on hers.

I remembered how my Sunday school teacher said we should pray for people who were sick or hurt. I had never done that before, but right then I prayed for my friend.

At first everyone was quiet. They were standing back because one of the firefighters told them to. But then the fireman who was helping my friend sat up, wiped his hand across his mouth, and shook his head. I heard the sound of more sirens and people beginning to cry and yell. Then an ambulance rushed up the driveway.

It was too much. I sank down in a corner and squeezed my eyes shut. I covered my ears to block everything out. I began to cry and to rock back and forth.

What had I done? I wanted it all to go away. I wanted my friend to get up off the ground. I wanted all these people to leave so that Foster Mom could call me to supper and I could take a bath and go to sleep in the room with my brothers.

But it didn't go away. Ever. The death of my friend was real. There was nothing anyone could do. Nothing I could do. And from the way I saw it, nothing even God could do.

Smoke inhalation.

They say it doesn't take much to kill a child.

They are fragile like that.

THAT WAS THE last day we saw Foster Mom and Dad.

When some of the neighbors found me in the garage, I

whispered to them what had happened. I told about lighting the candle and the dolls' houses catching on fire and me running away. I told them I was sorry. I told them I didn't mean it.

The neighbor took me by the hand and led me across the yard. When Foster Mom saw me, she grabbed me and hugged me. I remember feeling her arms around me, but I didn't hug her back. I couldn't raise my arms. It was like I was a rock or a piece of petrified wood.

When one of the neighbors told her what I had done, she let go of me and fell into Foster Dad's arms. He looked at me over her shoulder with his face all twisted up. He was crying. Then he cursed at me and told somebody they better take me somewhere far away. He wanted me out of his sight.

One of the firefighters told me to sit down on the grass and not move. My brothers came and sat beside me. Nobody spoke.

I wasn't crying then. People must have wondered why I was acting so calm. I know now I was probably in shock. I remember the words *she's dead* playing over and over again in my mind.

And I chewed on my knuckles until they bled.

THAT NIGHT WE went to an emergency shelter. Not Foster Mom and Dad—they stayed with friends. I learned later that the house was so badly damaged they had to tear it down.

It was my brothers and me who were sent to the shelter, and this time we stayed there for two weeks.

It was a long two weeks. I wasn't ever hungry, and I didn't want to play. I thought about the fire and about my friend every minute I was awake. Night after night I dreamed she was alive and everything was all right. After all, wasn't that what God was supposed to do—make sick and hurt people well? Waking up was terrible because it meant that everything was not okay and that it never would be.

We had been at the shelter for more than a week when somebody came to get me. I had to talk to this lady. She asked me how long I had been lighting fires. How many times had I done it?

The girl and I had lit the candle lots of times. So that's what I told her—"lots of times."

She wrote it down.

Then she asked me if I had ever hurt an animal. I told her that one time I had pulled Toby's tail.

"Only once?" she asked.

I said maybe twice.

She wrote that down too.

It's a given that homeless kids have problems. You are in the system, and people expect you to act out and to need special care. That's not all bad. But try having it in your record that you are a fire setter and a kid who is cruel to animals. That little piece of information pretty much seals the deal. Look it up. According to the books, fire setting and cruelty to animals are big red flags to anyone who works with troubled kids. They are seen as big-time predictors of future aberrant behavior.

It did not matter that I had been lighting a candle, not intentionally setting something on fire. And nobody asked me if I had pulled Toby's tail to be mean to him or only to catch him so I could pull him up into my lap and pet him between his ears until he licked me.

I was damaged goods. That's what my records indicated, and that's how I was already seeing myself.

After what happened, the social worker didn't even try to find foster homes for my brothers and me. There was no way anybody would take us. She picked us up at the shelter and told us we were going to a children's home a couple of hours away. None of us spoke much on the way. I sat in the middle in the backseat. My brothers had the windows.

"We're here, guys." The social worker steered through a big metal gate. I strained to see past my brother.

The children's home was on a hill. Lots of grass. No trees. All the buildings were red brick. A big one sat in the middle at the top of the hill. Other smaller, one-story buildings sat scattered below. They looked like regular houses, except they were all alike.

They called the little buildings cottages, and they were divided by age. So my brothers and I were separated. Again. There were ten kids to a cottage, one set of houseparents, and an aide who came in to help out during the day.

It did not take long to learn the routine. A bus picked us up in the mornings and took us to regular school. It brought us back in the evening. There would be a snack waiting for us. We would do homework if we had any, then our chores. Mine was emptying the trash cans into a bin beside the back door. After that I could go to the playground in the center of the hill and play with kids from the other cottages.

Every day I hurried to finish my chores so I could meet my brothers near the swings. Being in first grade I never had much homework, so I always got there first. Most days I got to see them but not always for very long. On Saturdays we did activities with the kids in our cottage. On Sundays we went to church. I got to see my brothers then too.

We went on that way for a couple of years. It wasn't like having a real family, but it wasn't a bad life. Not as good as living in the country but better than most of the foster homes.

Then one day, right after Christmas, my brother Sam and I were hanging out on the playground. We wore new sweatshirts—army green, with itchy tags. Somebody had donated a bunch of those for the kids who needed warm clothes.

"You want to throw the football?" I asked. My brother was teaching me how to spiral the ball.

"Not right now. I gotta talk to you about something." He picked up a stick and started digging in the ground. "Some people came to my cottage yesterday. A man and a lady."

"Who was it?"

"Their names are Linda and Ron. They've come a couple of times. They don't have any kids, but they want some. So they're thinking about adopting us."

"Are they nice?"

"I guess so." He kept digging in the dirt.

"How come I didn't see them?"

"I dunno."

"I bet I'll like them. Do they have any dogs?"

"One."

"That's good. And I hope they have a big TV. Are they picking us up?"

My brother wiped his nose on the back of his hand. "That's the problem. They can only take two kids. They said they didn't have enough room in their house to take three."

"So they can get a bigger house."

He threw the stick as far as it would go. "And right now they only want older kids."

"How old do you have to be?" I lifted my knuckle to my mouth.

"I don't know."

"I'll be eight in May."

"I don't think that's old enough."

I started to cry. "Maybe I can come when I'm nine."

"Maybe you can." He kept his eyes on the ground. "They're coming to get us tomorrow."

"So I don't get to go?"

He shook his head, and I forgot about wanting to throw the ball.

My housemother must have known what was going on. That night she came to sit on my bed and talk to me, but I turned away from her to face the wall. Words cannot express how lost and alone I felt then.

When she put her hand on my shoulder, I jerked away from her. I told her to leave me alone. When she tried to turn me over, I hit her. She was so shocked she didn't move, so I hit her two more times before she got up from my bed. I didn't care. I just wanted her to leave me alone.

The children's home was big on adoption. The goal was to find permanent homes for as many kids as possible. Three boys from my cottage had been adopted since I had been there. I shouldn't have been surprised that somebody wanted my brothers.

And I shouldn't have been surprised that nobody wanted me.

Who would? Everybody knew I was bad. I had heard the adults talk about what I had done. Most of the kids knew too. Some of them had done bad things but nothing as terrible as burning down a house and killing a kid.

I remembered hearing in church that God loved every-body. I didn't believe it. I was the reason my brothers and I had to leave the best place a kid could be. How could God love somebody like that?

The next day I said good-bye to my brothers.

I was seven years old.

OVER THE NEXT ten years I watched kid after kid get adopted out of my cottage, but there were a few who never got picked. Like the guy who had a big red scar on his face. And the boy who made weird noises and whose head jerked all the time. He couldn't help it, but no one wanted a kid like him.

And of course nobody wanted me.

We told each other and ourselves that we did not want to be adopted.

Right.

~~Like having a family who wanted us, who picked us out~~ from all the others, who was ready to take us home with them was something we were just too cool for.

Only once, when I was fourteen, did someone show interest in adopting me. It was this guy, Paul, and his wife, Sharon. We went on a walk together one day, just to talk and get to know each other. I liked them. I thought they liked me. It seemed like the walk went good. I remembered to say, "Yes, sir" and, "No, ma'am." I thanked them for the cookies they had brought. But when they found out about the fire and about the little girl getting killed, they said they were sorry. It wasn't going to work out.

When I got back from my meeting with Paul and Sharon, one of the guys in my cottage was playing Ping-Pong, wearing one of my shirts. He said it was his, but I didn't believe him. How stupid did he think I was? I was sure it was my shirt. I didn't like him lying to me, so I threw him down and started trying to tear it off him. I pulled on that shirt so hard, they told me later, I nearly choked the guy. I didn't care. He shouldn't have been messing with my stuff.

After a while it got to where I paid no attention to families coming to the children's home to meet us kids. I would get in trouble sometimes for not being polite. But really, what was the point? By this time I had lost track of my brothers. I was getting used to being all by myself in the world.

I got into lots of trouble for fighting. Not every day or even every week. Sometimes I would go months without getting into it with anybody. But then something would set me off. I'd get it in my head somebody was lying to me or not telling me the whole truth, and there I'd go; I'd be all up in somebody's face. They told me I needed to work on my anger issues.

It did not take long for people to learn to leave me alone . . . which, actually, was the whole point.

By the time I was in high school, I had learned to set the bar low. Expect nothing, get nothing—that was my motto. I asked little of other people and even less of myself.

College? Never gave it a thought.

Vocational school? Not for me, even though I had the grades for either one.

I graduated from high school three weeks after my eighteenth birthday. Two days after that, according to the state, I was no longer its concern.

The children's home had what they called an aftercare program. You were supposed to stay in contact after you aged out of the system. Counselors were available to talk to you and help you plan your future.

But I wanted no part of any of that. What kind of help could they give somebody like me? I had become a loner, and I wanted to be on my own. To make my own choices and to live by my own rules. Not to bother anyone and for nobody to bother me.

My plan was to get a job. Find a place to live. Buy a car.

But it was not that easy.

 Five

I HAD ALWAYS thought the way you found a job was to look in the newspaper. So that's what I did. I bought a paper out of the machine in front of the Quick Stop three days in a row. But I learned real fast that unless you were a nurse or a truck driver, you could forget about getting anything that paid much above minimum wage. And apartments cost a lot more than I expected. Nobody had ever told me about deposits. Three hundred dollars? Where was I supposed to get that? As for buying a car—don't even go there.

Before I knew better, I had hoped to work construction. No luck. In the end, all I could get was McDonald's—part-time. No way I could afford an apartment on what they paid me. So for months I worked during the day, hung out at the library until it closed, then slept in an all-night laundry.

The worst thing about that was the lights were on all night, and they played music. Country music, which has always made my head hurt. I never thought I would miss anything about the children's home, but I did miss having a real bed and a quiet, dark place to sleep.

The one good thing about the laundry was there was a

bathroom with a lock on the door. Plenty of hot water. Free soap. I cleaned up every morning in the sink before going to work—first at McDonald's, then Pizza Hut, then Home Depot.

It worked out okay until the laundry manager figured out I was spending the night there. She had the police throw me out. After that, I slept wherever I could.

A few nights a week I would snag a bed at a men's shelter. But I had to be there early to get a bed, and my shift at Home Depot did not end until after the doors were closed. Some nights a coworker would let me crash on his couch. Other nights I would sleep in the park.

This went on for eight or nine months. I was finally able to land a job in construction, though not doing any of the actual building. I was hired to clean up, pick up scrap lumber and other materials, and toss it all into an industrial-size Dumpster.

I tried to save some money, but I did not make all that much, so it was slow going. By the time I had a few hundred dollars put back, I was ready to get out of town.

I still wanted to do construction. I always liked working with my hands. So when I heard there were lots of construction jobs in a town that was an hour north, I hitched a ride, hoping to land a job and find a place to stay. This was in late March, and I guessed construction work would be gearing up soon.

The man who picked me up was a foreman for the city road department in the town where I was headed. Nice guy. He was heading back from visiting his grandkids. We got to talking. I asked him about construction work.

"No, not much of that. But if you're looking for work, I may be able to help you out. City's looking to hire a handful of seasonal workers for spring and summer. Might turn into something permanent. Most likely not. But the job would give you five or six months' work."

"What would I be doing?" I took a drink from the canned soda he had given me from the cooler between our seats.

"Mostly filling potholes, clearing debris from ditches, working as a flagman when parts of the road have to be closed down. It's hard, hot work, especially in summer—out in the sun all day."

"I don't mind that."

"Can you pass a drug test?"

"Yes, sir." We were getting close to town.

Before he let me out near downtown, he pointed out where I should show up if I wanted the job. He also pointed out a cheap motel close enough to walk to.

"Good luck, kid. Hope to see you Monday. Take care."

I hiked my way toward the motel. Place was one-story, brick, painted pink. Faded blue trim around the windows. It used to have a swimming pool, but it was full of dirt with some patchy grass growing in it. A few rusted metal chairs were leaned up against the side of the building. Cigarette butts were mixed in with dirt and gravel along the path toward the office.

The sign said they had vacancies. No kidding. The place looked deserted. About three cars was all.

I hated spending any of my cash on a motel. I wanted to save everything I possibly could for a down payment on an apartment. But I was smart enough to know I didn't know my way around town well enough to find a place to stay for free.

They had weekly rates. Cash only. The lady said the place was safe. She lived there full-time. And all the rooms had new locks.

I told her I would take a week and peeled off some bills. One thing was for sure—seven days, and I would be gone.

The room had a little refrigerator. No microwave, but the lady in the office said I could use the one there anytime I wanted. After I checked out the room, I went across the street for some food—beef jerky, popcorn, apples, frosted strawberry Pop-Tarts, and a six-pack of orange soda.

Back in the room, I took a shower, then stretched out on the bed. I turned on the TV, flipped through the channels. Went to sleep to Animal Planet. Woke up to the same thing, plus the smell of mildew and stale cigarettes coming from my pillow.

First thing I figured out when I went to see about the job was that I did not have the right kind of shoes. Everyone applying and everyone already working wore work boots. Dollar-store tennis shoes were not going to cut it.

That was more money I would have to spend—if I got the job.

Now I wasn't sure what to hope for. Sounds shortsighted now, but all I could think about then was how much work boots were going to cost and how every step I took moved me farther and farther away from getting a real place to stay.

All I wanted was somewhere to call home. Was that too much to ask? Other people had nice houses. I would have been happy with a crummy one-bedroom apartment. I wanted a place to put my stuff. A place where I could fix myself something to eat. A place I could sleep more than three nights in a row without worrying about getting kicked out or somebody coming in and messing with me.

Was it ever going to happen?

The interview process was not much. You had to pass a simple test and then take a leak in a cup. After that, they called you into a little office, sat you down, and asked you a few questions.

I looked at my feet. Thought about getting up and leaving right then.

The guy asking the questions pushed his glasses back up his nose. "New to town, I see."

"Yes, sir."

"Well, welcome. Good place to be. You got family here?"

"No, sir."

"Friends?"

"I keep to myself, sir."

He looked at me like he didn't understand. Then the phone rang, and that got him away from interrogating me. When he got off the phone, he signed his name to one of my forms. "Believe we've got a place for you, son, assuming you're willing to work. That and your drug test comes back clean."

It would.

Did I want this job? I eyed the door.

"'Course, you're going to need some boots. They sell 'em at the hardware store half a block east." He stood up to shake my hand. "Welcome aboard. Check back day after tomorrow. We'll let you know for sure. Oh, and best get you some good leather gloves while you're picking up your boots. This kind of work—you'll be needing them too."

BY THE TIME I showed up for my first day of work for the city, I was down to forty-seven dollars and two days of my paid-for week at the motel. All I could figure was I'd be spending every afternoon after work scrounging around for someplace safe to sleep that night.

There were five of us who started with the city mainte-nance department that week. I was the youngest. A couple of guys were in their twenties, another in his thirties. And one old man had to be fifty at least. Except for the old guy, they had all grown up nearby.

"Where you from?" they asked me that first day. We had been filling potholes all morning and had stopped in a shady area beside the road to eat our lunches.

I told them the name of the town I had left.

"Where you staying?"

I told them the motel, leaving off the fact that I would only be there two more nights. Then I pulled a novel out of my backpack, leaned up against a tree, and hoped they would take the hint. And everyone did, except for the crew foreman, Mike.

He wasn't the real foreman but an engineering student doing some kind of internship for college. Right now he was supposed to be out with the crews, supervising and learning the ropes. Once his regular semester was over, he would spend the summer working with the city engineer. That way he would be learning both sides of how things were done. Somebody said he was twenty-six, but he looked older. Tall. Really thin. Pale skin, like somebody who normally doesn't get outside enough. He always wore a ball cap over his reddish hair and smeared on sunscreen at every break, but he still kept getting burned.

He leaned over to get a look at the cover of my book. "Good book?"

I told him it was okay. It was an old western I had found in the dresser drawer at the motel. Nothing special.

"Like to read?"

"Sometimes." I turned the page.

"Me too. Used to, anyway." He pulled a leaf off a branch and began stripping it down to the vein. "Problem for me is with all the books required for school, I don't feel like reading."

I kept my eyes on the page. The guy was okay. Always checking to see if we had water and making sure we took breaks. But not so great at taking hints that somebody wanted to be left alone.

"You like it here?"

I gave up. Put my book back into my backpack and took a long swig from my water jug. "It's all right but not much in the way of cheap places to live." I had been looking in the papers. Most of the apartments were too nice for me. Pools. Clubhouses. Security. More than I could afford. What I wasn't seeing were halfway decent places with cheap rents.

"You looking for a place?"

"I was." No need to go into how I was broke until payday, which was two weeks away. "Not having much luck." Even if I found something, I did not have anything for a deposit. Even places that were dumps made you put something down for security.

"Don't know if you'd be interested, but my mom's got a room she rents out. Been empty going on a month."

"I was thinking I'd be getting an apartment."

"Don't blame you. But if you decide you're interested, you're welcome to come take a look. It's not like an apartment, but the room's got some privacy. It used to be the garage, but a few years back my dad converted it into a bedroom. It's separated from the main part of the house by a breezeway. No kitchen, but it's got its own bath."

He looked at his watch. Lunch break was over. "Let me know if you want to see it."

Nice of him to offer, but I was not interested in a room in some old lady's house.

At least not then.

Let's just say I became more interested after I spent three nights trying to sleep in an alley downtown and three mornings trying to clean up in the bathroom at Dairy Queen. I had given up the motel when I saw I was not going to be able to stay there and have money left for food. For five dollars the lady manager had let me leave my stuff in a storage closet inside the lobby for a few days. I had gone every morning to get clean clothes. So far, nothing had been stolen, but today it looked as if somebody had gone through my stuff. Maybe the manager, maybe someone else. I had to figure out something better.

"Mike, how much is your mom wanting for that room in her house? She still got it for rent?"

It was the end of the workday on Friday. The other guys had clocked out and were heading toward their trucks to go home to start their weekends. I held my time card in my hand. I was tired and hungry, and I could smell myself. All I could think of was how bad I missed taking hot showers. When you don't have anywhere to go, weekends are not your favorite part of the week.

I was ready to give up. Last place I had checked, rent was four-fifty, with a two-hundred-dollar deposit. May as well have been two thousand. Something had to give. I could not keep hanging out, waiting for something to happen so I could afford an apartment. Maybe living in an old lady's house wouldn't be so bad.

Mike shrugged. "Nobody's moved in, but she may have it promised. I'm heading home now. If you want, you can ride over with me and talk to her yourself."

"You live in the house too? With your mom and dad?" I had not thought of that. Mike wasn't exactly my boss, but he was sort of over me, at least for now. Living in his house with him and his parents might be weird. He was a college student, on the move up, and soon he'd be a big-shot engineer. I was just trying to lay low and get by, one day at a time. I wasn't so sure now about renting that room.

"Just my mom. My dad passed away six years ago." Mike turned off the lights. "She's cool. We get along, stay out of each other's way. So you want to take a look?"

Might as well.

The room was good. Great, actually. Furnished with a bed, a dresser, a desk, and lamps. No television, but I could live with that. Bathroom was small, but it had a shower. Hot and cold—I checked them both.

"I'm hoping you don't smoke." Mike's mom was showing me around. She'd said her name was Anna and for me to call her that. "But if you do, it's okay out here but not in your room." We were in the screened-in breezeway that ran between the room and the kitchen door of the main part of the house. There were a couple of wicker chairs and a little metal table. An old bicycle was leaned up against the wall.

"I don't smoke." She didn't need to know that I probably would if I could. The few times I had tried it, I liked the way smoking took the edge off. Truth was I could barely afford food. How could I buy cigarettes?

"Good. Come on into the kitchen." She was short, a little fat, looked to be about sixty, had a long braid down her back, wore jeans and a black T-shirt, and was barefoot. "Mike and I are pretty quiet, but we're easygoing. I don't mind you having friends over, even small parties now and then, as long as you keep things under control."

I almost laughed at that. "Not a problem," I told her.

I wanted the room, bad. I could already feel a pillow under my head and hot shower water on my back. Problem was, I was down to my last twenty dollars, and payday was a week away.

"Rent's two hundred a month. Mike told me you haven't been in town long, and I know it takes a while to get on your feet in a new place, so we'll skip a deposit. I just ask that you give me two months' notice if you decide to move out. Okay?"

I nodded. She stood there with her hands on her hips, looking at me over her glasses. "So, do you want to rent the room?"

"I'd really like to. Could you hold it a week?"

She pushed the glasses up on her nose. "You don't need it right now?"

Well, of course I did, but I wouldn't have the money until payday. I was wishing she wouldn't make me spell it out. I stumbled around, trying to figure out what to say. It didn't make sense, but I had a little bit of pride. "I'm in a little bit of a cash crunch."

She looked at me again and then nodded. "I think we can work around that. Room's empty, and it's going to stay empty till you move in. So it's no problem to me if you bring your stuff over today. We'll add an extra week's rent to whenever you move out. That sound fair?"

She had no idea.

"Works for me." I was so grateful that I did not know what to do. I should have said thank you, but I was so relieved, I forgot.

"Hey, Mike," she called. "Son, where are you?"

I hadn't even noticed that Mike had disappeared.

"Here, Mom. What do you need?" He ambled into the kitchen, opened the fridge, and grabbed an orange. "Want one?" He held it out to me.

"I'm good." I was in a hurry to go get my stuff. It would take me a good hour to walk to the motel, then another hour to get back to the house.

"Why don't you drive Josh to get his things. He's taking

the room, as of today. May as well get him moved in now. I'm going to start dinner."

"Hey. No. That's okay," I said. "I don't have that much. Really, it's not that far. It won't take me that long to walk over and get it."

"Nonsense." Anna started washing her hands at the sink. "Mike can take you."

Mike picked up his keys from the counter. "First thing you got to learn, living in the house with my mom: You may think you're just renting a room. You're not. Anybody my mom comes in contact with, she thinks she knows best, and they'll be better off if they do exactly what she says."

I did not like the sound of that.

Anna popped him in the rear with a rolled-up towel. "Don't listen to him. He's exaggerating. You're a grown man. I do not intend to interfere in your personal business."

I hoped not. All I wanted was the room. Privacy. No surprises. A safe place where I could close the door on everybody and everything, where I did not have to worry about people telling me I had done something wrong and making me go somewhere new.

"At least I won't be meddling all the time." She winked at me. "Now, go—both of you. And Mike, be back within an hour. I'm making meatballs."

Lucky Mike, I thought. Beef jerky and Pop-Tarts were on my dinner menu that night.

"So you've been on your own for a while?"

"Since I turned eighteen."

We were at the motel, and Mike was helping me load my stuff. Not that there was that much—just some clothes and my stash of food. If he wondered why my stuff was in a closet with cases of toilet paper and bottles of Lysol, he didn't let on.

"How old are you now?" he asked.

"Almost nineteen."

He shook his head. "I'm twenty-six years old, and I've never lived by myself."

I shrugged. If he liked living with his parents, that wasn't any of my business. And it wasn't like I had much of a choice in my living conditions.

"Sounds lame, I guess. I was set for college, even had some out-of-state coaches looking at me for basketball. Then right at the end of my senior year, I got sick. Cancer. That changed pretty much everything. I graduated, but there was no going off to college for me, and no college period for a couple of years. Then I could only go part-time at the school here in town. That's why I've still got three semesters to graduate after this one, counting this summer."

I didn't exactly know what to say to that, so I didn't say anything. He kept talking. "I lost my hair. My girlfriend too. She hung around for a while, came to see me when I was in the hospital, but then it got to be too much for her."

"Stinks." Why was he telling me all this? We were not exactly what you would call friends.

"Yeah, it does. But like they say, everything happens for a reason."

Not everything. At least not in my book.

"Almost two years of treatment, and I finally went into remission. Then my dad died. He and I were close. I mean, I've always been tight with both my parents, but my dad and I had something special. He was the best. When I was sick, he took off work all the time to be with me. He stayed with me day and night. When I lost my hair, he shaved his head too. When I threw up, he held the pan for me, then half the time he'd go to empty the pan and I'd hear him throwing up too."

He loaded the last box into his truck then walked around to open the door. "If I hadn't been sick, I would've probably been out of state, going to school, wrapped up in my own world. I'd have missed out on those last two years he had before his heart attack. When he died so suddenly, my mom needed me. With me just going to school part-time and commuting instead of living on campus, it's worked out. She didn't need to be alone."

"Sorry 'bout your dad." I wasn't used to somebody telling me their whole life story. But as long as Mike was talking about himself, we were not talking about me.

"Thanks."

"And the cancer? You're okay now?" Mike was skinny and really pale. Maybe he was still sick.

"Yeah, I'm fine now. Not cured exactly. I have to go for tests every six months, but so far so good." He put the truck in reverse.

Just goes to show—you never know about people. Here I thought Mike had it going on. But he had been real sick, and his dad had died, and Mike's cancer could come back. If that happened to me, I'd be real mad, but Mike seemed okay about it all.

Back home Mike parked close to the house. When we got out, I could smell the meatballs through the open kitchen window and hear Anna's off-key singing. She had the radio on, and she was singing along—belting it out. Mike grabbed a load and started to help me carry stuff in.

"I got it. Just set it down. I'll take what I've got in, then come back for the rest. Thanks for the ride." I headed toward the outside door that led to my room. "And hey, thanks for telling me about the room. I appreciate it. See you Monday."

"Monday?"

Today was Friday.

"You're not going to eat?"

"I've got stuff."

"You don't like meatballs?"

Well, sure I did. What was I supposed to say? I looked toward the door of my room, then back at Mike. What did he want from me? I was not company. I was not family. Enough was enough. I appreciated him helping me get the room, and I had told him thanks four times for taking me to get my stuff. Now I just wanted to take my gear to my room, close the door, and for the first time in my life, make myself at home in my own space.

"Oh man. Wait." Mike glanced over his shoulder toward the kitchen window. "Mom forgot to tell you, didn't she?"

Tell me what? I had my back to him, heading toward my room.

"The rent you're paying is not just for the room. You get dinner too."

I stopped, turned around, and faced him. "For two hundred dollars?"

"That's the deal. She always includes one meal a day in the price of the rent. Mom loves to feed people, and since there's no place to cook in the room, she figures that's fair. Nobody should have to go out for dinner every night. That's how she's done it with the other renters. 'Course, it's up to you." He motioned toward the bag of beef jerky sticking out of the box I was carrying. "If you'd rather have that, it's okay."

Beef jerky or meatballs. The choice was mine. Even if it meant enduring another hour of conversation, this was not a hard call. My stomach had been growling for the past half hour.

Meatballs it was.

 Six

ANNA HAD THIS chalkboard hung on the wall in the kitchen. Every day she printed what we were having for dinner that night.

Meatloaf.

Chicken stew.

Lasagna.

For dessert—pound cake.

Lemon squares.

And my all-time favorite, sweet potato pie.

How did Mike stay so skinny? I had rented my room for only a month when I had to buy bigger pants. I put my feet under Anna's table, and she put down platters and bowls of the best food I had ever eaten in my life.

Every night the three of us sat down to eat together. I felt out of place, sitting at the table with them. They were family. I was just some guy renting a room. But I guess that's not how they saw it because they never gave me an option.

Over dinner Anna would tell Mike and me all about her day. She worked mornings as a receptionist at a place where you go to donate blood. Afternoons, she worked in her organic garden, cleaned up the house, and made dinner. She loved to talk and was always cracking us up. You would not believe how many stories she came up with about a little bit of nothing. Whether it was garden compost, her latest crazy art project, or somebody who fainted while he was filling out his paperwork to give blood, she could make it sound interesting.

After she told us about her day, then she would ask Mike about his. And he would tell her about what he had done that day—who he had seen, what project the city was working on now, how it was progressing, and what was up next. He would talk about his supervisor and about the papers he was writing because of his internship. He asked her opinion about things too. If he had an issue with somebody on the crew, he would describe it and ask her what she thought.

They teased each other, going back and forth over little things, like the way Mike didn't like his food to touch or about how Anna's long hair made her look like an aging hippie.

"I am an old hippie. Sort of," Anna teased back. "And what's wrong with that?"

I had never been around a parent and a child who carried on like that. My parents didn't really talk to us. Foster parents talked more about us than to us. And there were too many of us in the children's home for the houseparents to spend much time talking to any of us. So all this talk was new to me.

It wasn't all teasing either. Often Anna would tell Mike how proud she was of him and how no matter what issue he was dealing with, she knew he would do the right thing. She would lay down her fork and put her hand on his arm, not to make him shut up and listen to her, but rather to let him know she was listening to him. She made it look like what he was saying was the most important thing she had heard all day.

Mike was under tons of pressure at work; he told me that lots of engineering students didn't make it through their internships. Especially after he finished his time with the road crew and began to spend his days with the city engineer, he would come home all balled up and tense. He didn't actually say it, but I figured out he was afraid he might not make it through. By the time we finished dinner, though, he was feeling better, looser, more sure of himself.

The way I saw it, what Anna was doing for Mike was holding up an imaginary mirror to him, making him look at himself the way she saw him. He was something good, somebody who could succeed at whatever he wanted to do. That is the picture she painted. I could see it. He could too.

The first couple of weeks, I just listened to the two of them talk. Occasionally they would try to include me, but I stayed quiet. I kept my eyes mostly on my plate, and they took the hint. But then something changed. I became a project or something. Dinner became Let's-see-if-we-can-get-Josh-to-talk-to-us time.

Anna would ask one question after another.

"What's your favorite baseball team?"

"How did you get that scar on your arm?"

"If you could have any car you wanted, what would you choose?"

I would answer each one quickly and go on with my meal. Not satisfied, she would take it up a notch.

When she passed me the potatoes: "Josh, you're an intelligent guy. What was your favorite subject in school? Ever think about taking some classes at the community college? I'd be happy to pick up some info for you if you'd like."

Between bites of smothered pork chops: "Hey, I like that shirt. Blue's a good color on you. When you were a kid, which crayon did you pick first from the box?"

As I bit into a buttered corn muffin: "You're welcome to use the computer in the living room anytime you want. Do you like to play games? I'm not very good on it, but if you need help, let me know."

And as I forked my last crumb of chocolate pie: "I've got the ironing board set up. Be happy to press something for you if you'd like for me to. Anything else I can help you do?"

The more Anna tried to get into my head, the more uncomfortable I felt. It got to where I dreaded dinner. Why wouldn't she leave me alone? If her meals hadn't been so amazingly good and if I hadn't always been starving after a day of manual labor, I would have skipped out on the food to avoid the interrogation.

Mike wasn't any better. I cannot tell you how hard it was not to pop off at him. His ways were not the same as Anna's, but they bugged me just as much. He wasn't bad about asking me stuff or telling me stuff, but he was always trying to give me rides to places. Trying to help me out in other ways too.

Without coming out and saying anything, I tried to show him I didn't need any help. But the guy could not take a hint.

When Anna told me I could use the bike that was in the breezeway, it became my main transportation. Occasionally I took Mike up on the offers for a ride—like when it was pouring down rain or when there wasn't any other way. But most mornings I biked to work even though Mike was going the same way in his truck. I made excuses, told him I had to clock in early, or I had to stop by the store on the way home. He knew I was making stuff up, but he never acted mad or anything, just kept on offering to help me out.

It might sound weird that something like that would bug me. But I had not signed up for a friend.

Or a mother.

Anna thought she was helping me the way she helped Mike. But you know that mirror she held up to help him remember who he really was? That was the last thing I wanted.

I did not need to be reminded of who I was.

Some things are impossible to forget.

A few weeks into all this, I came up with what I thought was a great plan. I went to the dollar store and bought some paper plates, some plastic forks, and some throwaway cups. I didn't think it would be a big deal.

I was wrong. I will never forget the look on Anna's face.

She had made chicken potpie that night. And salad. And cherry cobbler for dessert. I showed up in the kitchen at six thirty as always. But instead of sitting down, I held out my paper plate for her to see. "If it's okay, I'm going to fix my plate and take it back to my room."

"I'm sorry?" She didn't understand.

"I'm kinda tired," I lied. "I thought I'd make my plate and go relax in my room. Save you from washing my dishes."

She could not hide her surprise. Or her hurt. But she tried to. "Oh. Okay. Sure. That'll be fine." She fumbled with the spoon in the potpie, dropped the spoon on the floor, picked it up, and burned herself on the edge of the pan.

"You okay?"

"Of course. Uh, let's see." She ran her burned finger under the cold water. "There's a tray up in the top of that cabinet. The one to the left. You can use that to carry your food. No need to make two trips."

I retrieved the tray. I knew I was being a jerk, but I didn't care enough to back down.

"Salt and pepper," she said, handing me a pair of shakers out of the cupboard. "These are extra. Take them. I know how it is. You've got to taste your food before you know if it's seasoned like you like it. And here are some napkins. Anything else?" She faked a smile.

"No. This is good."

Just then Mike walked in. He looked at me with my tray of food. "Hey, where you going?"

I opened my mouth to say something, but Anna interrupted. She motioned for me to go on. "Did you bring in the newspaper? Mind going back out for it, please?"

Mike just stood there, but I hoofed it back to my room.

Which is where I ate from then on.

I still rode with Mike when I had to, still spoke to Anna from time to time, but mostly I paid my rent and stayed to myself. And they left me alone, which was exactly the way I wanted things.

I had just turned nineteen. According to the state, I did not need a parent.

I did not need anyone.

Or so I thought.

 Seven

A MONTH OR so after I started eating in my room, I woke up one morning before my alarm went off. I was shivering and shaking even though it was summer and the air conditioner in my room didn't work all that great. Then I broke out in a cold sweat. The nausea hit right at the same time as the gut cramps.

I did not make it all the way to the bathroom.

And for the first time in my life, I was so sick I didn't care.

I thought I was going to die. Every joint in my body hurt. My mouth was so dry my tongue felt cracked. When I stood up, the room spun and my knees buckled. I was freezing to death, but all I had in my room was one blanket and one quilt. I stumbled around, put on some sweatpants and a long-sleeved shirt, then curled up in my bed until my teeth quit chattering and I fell asleep.

I had no idea whether it was day or night when I woke up and heard Anna hollering and knocking on my door. I tried to tell her to come on in, but no sound came out when I tried to yell. She knocked and knocked, then tried the door.

Of course I had it locked.

The knocking stopped, but in a few minutes I heard her back outside my door. She was talking to Mike.

"He never showed up at work is what they said."

"And you didn't call to see if something was wrong?" I heard keys jangling.

"Mom. I was in the office all day. I didn't realize Josh wasn't at work until after three. I figured he'd just decided to take a day off."

"Did he call in?"

"Crew manager said he didn't hear a word from him."

"Something's wrong. You know Josh wouldn't just not show up."

I heard a key in the lock.

"You shouldn't just barge in, Mom. Wait—this isn't right. It's his room. Mike likes his privacy."

"It may be his room, but it's my house, and I'm going in. Something's wrong. I know it."

She pushed open the door. Mike was behind her. Forget privacy. I was so glad somebody was there I didn't know what to do. I was embarrassed for them to see me in bed. Ashamed of the mess. But mostly I was relieved I wasn't alone.

"Josh, what's wrong?" Anna put her hand on my head. "You're burning up with fever."

I tried to sit up.

"When did you get sick? Have you been here all day?"

I tried to say something, but nothing came out.

"Honey, we've got to get some fluids in you. Have you taken anything for that fever?"

I shook my head.

"No. Of course you haven't. Mike, go get some Tylenol. And a big glass of Sprite."

She sat down on the edge of the bed. "You're dehydrated."

She glanced toward the bathroom. "How many times have you thrown up?"

I held up five fingers.

"Is your throat sore?"

I nodded again.

Josh brought a Sprite over ice and set it on the table. Anna shook two Tylenol out into my hand. I swallowed both, but they did not stay down long. At least this time I made it to the bathroom—which Mike had just finished cleaning up. He was standing next to the toilet, holding a can of Lysol spray. When he saw me coming, he got out of the way quick.

When I was done, he handed me a wet washcloth.

"Sorry," I mouthed. I was sitting on the edge of the tub, waiting for the next round.

"No problem, man. Doesn't bother me a bit. When I had chemo, lots of people cleaned up after me. Feel any better?"

I leaned over the toilet again. Nothing but dry heaves.

Anna was standing in the doorway. "You need to see a doctor. Maybe get an IV. There's an urgent-care center other side of town. And let's get you a trash can. You know. Just in case."

"No, I'm okay." I was on my knees in front of the toilet again.

"Sure you are. That's why you're bowing to the great porcelain god. Come on, now. You're going."

"I don't have money for a doctor. No insurance. I'll be all right." The actual truth was I had eight hundred dollars in my bottom drawer. I was saving for a car. What can I say? My priorities have not always been in the right order.

Anna moved to help me up. "Sorry. I'm pulling rank on you, bud. Doctor visit cheaper than a funeral."

"Mom, don't say that."

"I'm serious." She got on one side to help me up. Mike got

on the other. I hadn't had a shower, and I was so rank I could smell myself, but neither of them let on. They helped me put on shoes and a clean shirt since the one I was wearing had spots of puke on it.

Who knew you could get the flu in June? That's what the doctor said I had. He also said it was a good thing Anna made me come in. We were at the urgent-care center for four hours while they did tests and gave me medicine and IVs.

When they finally told us it was okay to go, I was afraid of what was coming next. How was I going to pay for it all? How much had it cost?

I never found out.

I also never found out how much the prescriptions Anna got filled for me cost.

Later I got to feeling guilty about my secret savings. It wasn't right for me not to pay for the doctor and medicine when I really did have the money, even if it meant killing my dream of owning a car. I asked Anna how much I owed her, but she told me it had been taken care of. I asked her several times, but she wouldn't say.

"It's not right for you to do something like that for me. I know it cost a lot."

"Not so much."

We both knew that was not true.

"I'll pay you back."

"No, don't do that. Wait until times are better for you; then do the same thing for somebody else. That's how you can pay me back."

This wasn't right. Nobody did stuff for other people without expecting something back. Not in my world. "When I get on my feet, I'll—"

Anna put her hand on my arm. "Stop. Don't say another

word. It's what people do. We help each other. People have helped me when I needed it, so when I can, I do something for you. Then you pass it on to somebody else." She grinned. "Come on. You're a smart guy. It's not that hard to understand."

She had no idea.

After I got home from the urgent-care clinic, Anna checked on me every few hours. She brought me nasty-tasting herbal tea that she said was good for my immune system. She reminded me to take my medicine.

"You feel like you can eat something?" I had gone most of the evening without feeling like I was going to throw up.

"Maybe."

She brought me chicken noodle soup, crackers, and apple-sauce on a tray. "Not too much too fast. Just a little at a time."

Mike brought me a couple of novels he had already read. He eyed the tray. "That's what Mom always made for me when I was sick when I was little. And later, when I'd be sick from the chemo." He looked to see that she wasn't in the room. "Word to the wise. She'll try to convince you not to eat anything but those three foods for the next three days. You're gonna be sick of 'em. When you're hungry for something else, give me the heads-up, and I'll make you a burger run. She'll never know."

I was worried about missing work. I had been so sick that first day I had not called in. What if I lost my job? But when I called and talked to my boss, he told me it was okay. Mike had told them what was going on. I was still worried. I was losing money every day I was out, but at least I still had my job.

When I had to go back to the doctor for a follow-up, Mike drove me. On the third day I was still feeling rotten but better enough to get bored. Mike got the TV from his room and set it up so I could watch it from my bed. Anna did not watch

TV, so considering his was the only set in the house, that was a pretty nice thing for him to do.

The flu takes a lot out of you. It was a good week before I was well. But by the fourth day, I was feeling good enough to get up and get dressed.

And come to the table for dinner.

I had eaten my last meal in my room.

 Eight

ANYBODY WHO'S EVER had the flu will think I'm crazy saying this, but getting sick turned out to be the best thing to happen to me in a long time. It shook me awake.

I don't know what I had been thinking. Avoiding Mike and Anna. Eating in my room. Treating them like they had done something to me when all along they had been trying to do something *for* me. All I know is that having them taking care of me when I was nothing to them—when I had treated them so badly—tore down something inside me. It opened me up. Made me see myself differently from what I had seen before.

Maybe I wasn't as much of a loner as I had liked to think I was.

I had not been worth much to my own family, but for some reason it seemed I was worth something to these strangers. Perhaps they saw something in me that my own parents missed. I toyed with the belief that my parents had been wrong about me and that Mike and Anna were right in thinking I was someone who mattered.

Any rate, I started spending a lot more time with them.

A couple of times a week, I hung out with Mike. We shot

hoops in the driveway even though he could not play for long before getting winded and having to sit down. I pretended not to notice, but it was obvious to me Mike was not in very good shape. Or maybe I was in better shape than he was because I did outside work and he was now spending his days in the office with the engineer.

On Friday nights Mike and Anna and I would watch a movie on his little TV. I would lie back in an old bean bag chair, look over at the two of them laughing and eating popcorn, and wonder how I got to be where I was.

On weekends Mike taught me how to cook steaks and burgers on the grill. "If you're looking, you're not cooking. Keep the lid down. Don't turn your burgers more than once. Those are the secrets," he told me about grilling.

Anna liked it when we cooked out because that meant she did not have to heat up the kitchen. Those nights were the best. We ate at the picnic table on the back deck. First we would chow down till we were full; then we would lean back in lawn chairs and look up at the night sky. We would go long minutes without anybody saying anything, all of us just staring up into that blackness, into all those stars, just like I had done back at the foster home. I had come so far it was hard to believe it was the same sky as back then.

I know. All this sounds like nothing special. Three people sharing meals, sitting outside together, not saying much. But here's the thing. The way Anna and Mike treated me, like I was somebody worth something, like I was valuable for just being—well, it was like a big ripped-up piece of me was coming together.

I will be honest, though. Sometimes the good feelings I got from them scared me. Letting down my guard was not an easy thing. But it was a good thing.

Things were going pretty good at work, though there had been a couple of close calls. This one guy on the crew knew how to push my buttons, and I had nearly gotten into it with him a couple of times. Luckily, both times there had been other guys around, and they had helped me cool off before things got bad. Looking back, I don't know what I was thinking. I needed this job.

Anyway, with a steady job and a place to live, my life settled into a routine. During the week Mike and I would get home from work a few minutes after five. We would do a few chores around the house to help Anna out, and then I would go to my room to clean up. Later the three of us would have dinner at the kitchen table. After we were finished, Mike would go to his room to work on stuff for his internship.

At first I would go back to my room too. But then I got into the habit of staying in the kitchen with Anna, helping her clean up. She had a dishwasher, but she didn't like to use it. So it got to be my job to wash the dishes while she put the food and stuff away. Night after night Anna and I worked side by side in that kitchen.

Some nights I would feel like talking, some nights not. Usually Anna was cool about that. But other times her interest in my life made me clam up. I would tell her stuff, then feel like I had said too much.

One night I told her about my parents getting killed, about being in foster care, and about growing up in the children's home. I talked about turning eighteen and leaving the home, how hard it was to make a living. I described what it had been like when I first moved to town, how I stayed at the motel, then had to sleep in the alley. About running out of money and having to wash up for work in the bathroom at Dairy Queen.

Anna was wiping down the stove. "Not many people I know would have figured out how to survive the way you did."

"It wasn't such a big deal."

"You are one of the most resilient guys I've met. Mike and I have learned a lot from you about courage and strength."

I felt embarrassed when she said that, but proud too.

One night, a week or so later, I was washing, and Anna was drying. We'd had nachos that night. I kept missing spots of stuck-on cheese, and Anna kept sending the dishes back for me to give them another swipe with my rag. And I wasn't in the best mood to start with. Some guy at work had ticked me off, and I had not been able to shake it. So every time she handed a plate back, I got a little bit more irritated. "Sorry. I've never been the best at washing dishes."

"Did you have chores at the children's home?"

"Yeah, everybody did. But there were so many of us, nobody had to do too much."

"So how long were you in foster care before you went to the children's home?"

"I don't know. A couple of years. Maybe three." I didn't like where this conversation was going. I was not in the mood.

"Which was better, foster care or the children's home?"

"Foster care." I handed her a plate. Time to change the subject. "Man, those were some hot peppers we had tonight. My mouth is still burning."

Anna was not taking the hint.

"Were you with your brothers in foster care?"

"The last one. Yeah. We were together in the last one."

"And you liked it? You liked the family?"

"They were okay."

We were finished with the dishes. Anna rinsed out the sink. I lifted the overflowing bag out of the kitchen trash can to take it to the can out back. I had made it to the back door when the side of it ripped and trash spilled onto the floor and onto my bare foot. Grease. Coffee grounds. Wadded-up paper towels.

Wiping down the counters, her back to me, Anna didn't see the spill. She just kept on with her questions. "I bet you miss your brothers. You keep in touch?"

I cursed. "No. I don't. I don't know where they are. They don't know where I am." I was yelling. "Can you get off my back for just one minute? Can't you see I'm trying to clean up this mess?"

Anna laid her dish towel on the counter and turned to look at me. I kept my eyes focused on the trash. She moved to help, but I pushed her away. "I got it." I scooped up the trash with my hands, shoved it in the bag, and took it out the back door, down the steps, and across the yard to the can.

When I came back inside, Anna was sweeping up what I had missed. For a long moment, neither one of us spoke.

I gave in first. "I'm sorry. I didn't mean to yell at you. Dinner was good. Everything's okay. I'm calling it a night."

"Wouldn't it be great if you reconnected with your brothers?"

I clenched my jaw. "No. It wouldn't. Trust me."

"Oh, come on. I could help you."

I'd had all I could take. "Look, something happened. Something bad. Something you do not want to know about."

"Try me."

Anger rose in my throat the way acid does when you're about to throw up. "We were together in foster care. We were living with nice people. We were happy. But then I screwed up bad, and all of us had to leave. We had to go to the children's home. That's what happened. End of story."

"You were a kid. What could you have done that was so bad?"

"You're not hearing me. I don't want to see my brothers. They don't want to see me. It was a bad, bad scene. My brothers got adopted. I didn't. We lost touch. Sam and Matt—can you believe it? I don't even know their last names. I don't know where they live. I don't know anything about them. And I don't want them to know anything about me either. They're better off. That's why I changed my name when I came here. Everybody here knows me as Josh, but legally I'm Justin."

Anna looked at me with surprised eyes. "I'm sorry. I asked too many questions. Forgive me. But I have to say this—I don't believe it's better for you not to be in contact with your brothers. I bet they'd love to hear from you. And I could help. I know this woman who has helped a lot of people connect with lost relatives."

I swallowed. My throat felt full, as if I were trying to swallow the towel in Anna's hand. She was not going to give this up. "No."

"Give me one good reason."

I lost it. "One good reason? You really want to know the reason?" You can only push a person so far, and Anna had pushed me past the point of no return. I was so mad I started bawling. Good thing. If I had not started crying, I might have started hitting. Tears and snot were running down my face. "You think I'm this regular person with regular problems that you can fix. Well, I'm not."

"Josh." She tried to hug me, but I wouldn't let her.

Everything I had held back for so long got released. I was talking so fast I'm surprised she could understand my words. I told her all of it. Every detail. "There was a little girl. We played together every day. She was my friend. And I killed her."

I did not dare look at Anna's face, just kept blurting out the story. The matches and the fire. Running away and hiding. Watching the firefighters carry my friend out of the house. "They found her in my room. They tried, but they couldn't save her. She died from the smoke."

I held my head in my hands. It was too much. Why had she pushed me to tell her? Why? I was so mad. Mad at her. Mad at myself. Mad at the world.

"Josh, tell me. How old were you when it happened?"

"Six." I didn't look up.

"You were a child yourself. It was an accident. You know that, don't you? You aren't to blame."

I wouldn't look at her. "Don't you get it? It doesn't matter how old I was. It's my fault she died. I will always be to blame."

"Did you decide that yourself, or did someone tell you to carry this thing?"

How could she ask me that? "No one had to tell me. I just knew. And that's not the only thing that's my fault. The fire is why we had to go to the children's home. Not just me. My brothers had to leave the foster home, and they hadn't done anything wrong. They were happy. We all were. And we were together before I messed everything up.

"At the home everyone knew I was the kid who set the fire. I was the one who murdered a little girl. When people came looking for a kid to adopt, they never looked at me because I was the boy who started fires. That's why I never got adopted." I reached for a paper towel to wipe up my snot. When it didn't tear off easily, I yanked it so hard the holder pulled loose from the wall. "Not that I blame them. Who'd want a kid like me around?"

"I would."

I shook my head. She did not know what she was saying.

Anna's hand was on my shoulder. She turned me around

so we were standing face-to-face. She stood there, not saying anything until I looked up. I felt like I was ten years old. I wanted to pull away, but her eyes locked onto mine. "Josh, you did not mean for that little girl to die. You have convinced yourself that you're damaged goods because of something you did when you were little, but you're wrong. Terrible things have happened in your life. But the fact that you're still here on this earth means that you are strong. You have courage. You've survived things in your life that would have caused most people to give up. But you didn't. You kept living."

She moved her hand from my shoulder and took both my hands in hers. I looked up at her, then away again.

"You don't have to keep paying for what you did. It doesn't work that way."

"You don't understand. She was special. Innocent. I can close my eyes and see her. I never want to forget her, what I did to her, how she died."

Anna's chin wrinkled. She bit her lip. "Don't forget her, Josh. Remember her—forever. But remember how she lived, not how she died. Okay? Just do that. Try. It's the best thing you can do."

I nodded, though I wasn't ready to do what she said.

Anna let go of my hands and turned away from me. I saw her lift the dish towel to her face to wipe her eyes. Then she laid it back down on the counter but kept her back to me. "I'm pretty tired, Josh. Let's call it a night."

Fine by me. It was only eight, but it felt like midnight. I wanted to go to my room and never come out.

Anna still didn't face me. "Think about what I said. I'm here for you if you want to talk about this some more. Later."

I told her okay.

But I knew I never would.

 Nine

DINNER WAS ENCHILADAS, guacamole, and Anna's famous homemade salsa—which was major hot. I washed it down with iced tea. "How much longer till you graduate?" Mike had been complaining about how much schoolwork he'd have once the fall semester started.

"If I pass everything, I'll finish up next May."

"That's not so long." Like I was any kind of authority on college life.

Anna scooped some guacamole onto a chip. "You ever think about college, Josh?"

"Nope. Never."

"What did you want to be when you were a kid?" Mike wiped salsa off of his chin.

"Never thought about being anything. Just planned on getting a job. Making money. Getting by."

"Nothing wrong with working at a job," said Anna. "But if you were ever interested in doing something else, community college is a great place to start. Tuition's not too steep. Counselors are helpful. Classes are small, and they offer lots of them at night. I took some classes a couple of years ago—art appreciation and English literature. Enjoyed them, so I'm thinking about taking a couple more classes in the fall."

"Can you do that? Take random classes?"

"Sure. They have to ask you what you're wanting to do, and they make you up some kind of a plan. But you still get to take classes, whether you follow that plan or not. What would you be interested in taking?"

I thought about it. "Astronomy, maybe. I like looking at the stars."

The next evening, when I came into the kitchen, Anna was stirring gravy on the stove. She pointed to a packet on the table. "I went by the college today. Picked up a catalog and admissions paperwork for both of us. I'm thinking I'd like to take sociology, maybe world history. They've got astronomy on the fall schedule. I looked. You should do it."

I sat down at my place at the table and looked at the stuff. College? Me? That would be a trip. "You think they teach you to use telescopes? Or is it all studying stars in books?"

Anna turned the fire down under the gravy. She picked up the catalog and thumbed through it. "I don't know. Let's see if it tells." She pushed her glasses up on her nose. "Here's where the astronomy classes are listed. There are two different ones. And they both have labs that meet at nine o'clock at night."

Labs? What was that supposed to mean?

"So I'd say you study from books during class, and then study the real things on lab nights. And probably, yes, with telescopes would be my guess."

Cool.

ENROLLING IN COLLEGE wasn't as big a deal as I thought it would be. Before I started, I had to take some placement tests in math and reading. I was pretty nervous about that, but turned out I was not as dumb as I thought. Once I was accepted, I signed up to take two fall classes—basic astronomy and English composition. The counselor talked me into going with the English. She said if I ever did decide I wanted to work on a degree, I would have to have it.

Not only did I start college that fall; I finally got a car. Paid two thousand dollars cash for it. Don't ask me how I saved that much money. I still can't believe I did it on what I was making. I have to admit it was hard to hand over all that hard-earned cash. But the city had decided to keep me on at work on a month-to-month basis, at least through the fall, so I figured I could probably swing it.

Having my own wheels meant no more biking in the rain because I was too proud to accept a ride from somebody. It meant I could get to class in ten minutes instead of an hour. I got an extra forty-five minutes' sleep every workday because I could make it to work in no time.

Having a car was more than transportation. It meant dignity and freedom.

Things that had been in short supply most all of my life.

BY LATE NOVEMBER I was pretty sure I was going to make an A in astronomy and a B in English. I went ahead and signed up for two classes to begin after the holidays. Things had slowed way down at work, and about half the crew got laid off until spring. When my boss called me into the office, I knew I was getting cut too. Shoot. What was I going to do now?

"Have a seat, Josh." He leaned back in his chair, across the desk from me. "Everything going okay for you?"

"Yes, sir." *Get to the point. Don't make this harder for me than it already is.*

"You've done a good job for the city. You're a hard worker. Been on the road crew going on a year now; am I right?"

More like eight months, but I nodded. "Yes, sir. I was hired on for seasonal, but I made it through the last couple of cuts."

"I've got a proposition for you if you're interested."

What was he talking about?

"A position has opened up at the water-treatment plant. It's a good job. Good raise from what you're making and a chance to move up even farther in a few months if you do well. Your attendance record is excellent. You hardly ever call in sick, so you've got a few days of time off built up. Since you'll still be employed with the city, all that will carry over. Are you interested?"

"Yes, sir, I'm very interested. When would I start?"

"Not sure exactly. There's just one problem."

Uh-oh. I knew it. Too good to be true.

But it wasn't.

"We're going to miss you here." He stood up to shake my hand. "I'll have a hard time finding another worker as good as you. You're strong and dependable and a good problem solver."

"Thank you, sir." I wanted to tell him filling potholes and trimming medians was not exactly rocket science, but I kept that to myself.

"Good luck, son. You're going to do well."

After all the bad luck in my past, it looked like parts of my life were turning around. And I had managed to control my temper on the job, which had not always been easy. My new job was so much better than my old one. I could not believe the raise I got. I was actually making enough to afford a nice apartment, if I decided that was what I wanted to do. In the meantime, I started saving nearly half my check.

CHRISTMAS WAS A couple of weeks away. "So, we getting the tree today?" Mike was chewing on a piece of toast.

Anna poured herself a cup of coffee. "You sure you're feeling like it?"

Mike was getting over a bad cold, and he still had a cough. "Yeah, I'm okay."

"We don't have to go today."

"Sure we do." Today was Saturday. "If we don't get it today, then when will we?" Mike's voice was a little hoarse.

"I don't like the sound of that cough."

Mike wasn't taking the hint, so I tried to help Anna out. "What's the big deal?" I said. "You go down to Walmart and pick out a tree. I can go get one if you want, long as it will fit on the top of my car. How tall a tree should I get?"

Mike laughed. "Buy a tree from a lot? Nope. Not in this family you don't. Mom has to have fresh. As in cut-it-yourself-tree-farm fresh."

Anna put her cup down. "I don't know. Maybe this year—"

Mike interrupted. "Mom, we're going. After lunch. Okay?"

The trip to the tree farm was a new experience for me. First we got on this hay wagon. A tractor pulled it and us out into the areas where the trees were big enough to cut. We tramped through the rows and rows of trees. They all looked the same to me but not to Anna. One was too full. One was too flat. She was like a kid, hurrying from one tree to the next, sure it was better than the one we had just passed.

"This is it. This is the one. Don't you two agree?" She

was standing beside a nice one, checking all around it for bare spots.

"Perfect, Mom. Just perfect."

"Josh, you want to do the honors?"

What honors?

She handed me the saw.

Nineteen years old and I had never before cut down a Christmas tree. The first four years of my life, we did not even have a tree.

I made the cut all the way through. "Timmm-berrr!" Then we loaded it onto the trailer, and the guy drove us in to where we paid. Sixty dollars for a tree you cut yourself.

Getting the tree was a big holiday tradition for Anna and Mike. Church at Christmas was a big deal, too, but I had no intention of getting involved in that. Mike and Anna had invited me to their church a few times, but I hadn't gone. I was glad they did not hassle me about it.

Saturday before Christmas, when I came to the kitchen for dinner, Anna was pulling pans of cookies out of the oven. She was also singing along with the radio station that played holiday music 24/7.

"Okay, Josh," she said when she saw me, "here's the deal. There's a special service at church tomorrow. I think you'd enjoy it. Would you come? Please? It would make me so happy to have you and Mike both there."

She had made my favorite cookies—chocolate chip. I snagged one from the pan, bit into it, and burned my tongue. "What time's it start?"

"Seven."

"I don't have any dress-up clothes."

"No problem. This service is casual."

"Jeans?"

"Perfect. So you'll go?"

"I guess so. Yeah. Sure." I could do this for her. It was Christmas, after all. Goodwill toward men and all that.

Ladies too.

As we walked up the sidewalk, I could hear music coming from the open doors of the church. Voices. Guitars. A couple of guys stood outside, handing out candles with little plastic cones around them to catch the wax that would drip when they were lit. Anna had not told me the service would be by candlelight.

I felt my pits start to sweat. When the guy tried to give me a candle, I passed and was grateful nobody made a big deal of it. I had no intention of ever holding another candle in my hand.

Anna headed down the aisle to a place about halfway down. She eased in, and Mike followed, then me, and some other people. But we didn't sit down. Everyone was standing up.

After a couple of songs, the minister told us to take our seats. The only light was from a row of candles on the altar. I tried not to look, but my eyes kept going back to them. Once the music stopped, everyone sat quietly, even the kids. The air in the room felt heavy. People coughed. A lady next to us opened a peppermint. A little girl two rows down laid her head on her mother's shoulder. My mouth felt dry.

The minister stood up and began to read from the book of Luke.

I had heard the story before, of course, when my foster parents took us to church and then at the children's home. I knew how to behave in church. The hymns and stuff were familiar and even a little comforting.

I just was not buying any of it.

All those times at church I had heard that God loved us. That he loved everyone in the world. That he answered prayers. At one time I had even been on the verge of believing in all that. But then the fire happened. I had asked God to help out then, and look what he did.

Nope. No more counting on God—or anyone else, for that matter.

I glanced over at Mike, at Anna on the other side of him. Anna looked back in my direction, caught my eye, and smiled.

One thing about Anna, it was no act.

When it was time to pray, we bowed our heads. I did not close my eyes.

After the guy said amen, a guitarist began to play, and the moment I feared arrived. The minister lit the candle of the lady on the end of the first row. She lit the one of the person on her left.

I watched the progression move closer and closer to our row. One candle after another. One flame after another. The more candles were lit, the warmer the room got until I couldn't take it anymore.

I was out of there.

I stepped on a half dozen feet when I cleared the pew, but I didn't care. I needed air.

And I needed to throw up.

Mike found me around the side of the entrance, tossing my cookies into the bushes. Good thing it was dark. He stood and waited until I was through.

"You okay?" He handed me a tissue.

"Yeah. Just got hot. Needed some air. Sorry. You're missing the end of the service."

"No prob." He pointed to a side door just down from

where we were. It was almost over. "I'm not going back in. Want to hang here until it's over?"

The cool concrete steps felt good. We could hear the congregation singing through the open back door. I wasn't the only person who had gotten hot.

"What'd you think of the service?"

"Nice. Musicians are good. People seem friendly."

Pretty soon the music stopped, and it got quiet. I figured they were having a prayer. Then we could hear everyone talking, and through the window we saw that they had turned on the lights.

"Want to go back in? They're serving cookies and hot chocolate in the fellowship hall."

If the lights were on in the building, I figured I was safe from the candles. "Think I'll pass on the cookies, but I could use something to drink."

Back inside a ton of people came up to shake my hand and tell me how glad they were I had come. If any of them had seen my fast exit, they were nice enough not to say anything. Anna dragged me from person to person, telling them all about me, how I had a new job, how I was in school, and how glad she and Mike were to have me renting their room. I met the minister and a handful of Mike's friends.

After we got past the candles, it was all good.

On the way home, Anna and Mike chatted in the front seat. I looked out the window and up into the dark night sky.

For so many years, there had been no light in my life. No light from my parents. No light after them—not really. Until Anna. And Mike.

I was a long way from being brilliantly lit, but I was beginning to feel a small glimmer of something that might turn out to be light.

 Ten

CHRISTMAS EVE, WE stayed up till midnight playing Mexican Train, which is this domino game that Anna loved. We played about a dozen rounds and ate about a dozen Christmas cookies each.

"Guys, that's it for me. I'm heading to bed." Anna yawned and stretched.

Mike shoved the dominoes into the box. "Me too."

"Wait a second." I pulled two envelopes out of my back pocket. "I want to give you these now. Merry Christmas." I hadn't known what to get them, so I had picked up a couple of gift cards.

Anna opened hers. "This is great! Bath & Body Works. Thanks, Josh."

Mike's was from Best Buy. "Thanks, buddy. I can think of about half a dozen things I can spend this on."

"You're welcome. Wish it was more. I hope you guys have a great day tomorrow. I'll see you on Monday."

"What do you mean Monday? You going somewhere?"

"Maybe. I've got stuff to do."

We all knew I was lying. What does anyone have to do

on Christmas Day other than spend time with their families, doing family stuff? It just didn't feel right to me to be barging in on their family Christmas.

"Too bad. Your stuff will have to wait. You're having breakfast with us," said Anna. "Lunch too. See you back here in the morning—nine o'clock. One Christmas tradition that's different from when Mike was a kid is that we sleep in. So see you then. No discussion. Got it?"

I told her I did.

Lying in bed that night, I thought of past Christmas Eves. In foster care, the kids usually all got the same thing—like sweatshirts, candy, and a toy or a game, usually bought by a charity or the fire department or something. At the children's home, the houseparents got the week of Christmas off so they could be with their real families. Most kids left during that week too. If they had an aunt or a grandparent, they would go stay with them, and some kids had actual parents who for some reason could not take care of them during the year. Those of us who did not have anyone to take us would be consolidated into one or two cottages, and substitute houseparents would take care of us. I guess they paid them extra or something. Maybe time and a half.

The first couple of years were good because Sam and Matt and I got to be together. But after they got adopted, Christmas was just a long week to get through. I would miss the guys in my cottage and wonder what they were doing. With no school and not many of us left, there wasn't much going on. Normally we were on a strict schedule, but that week we just hung out. They let us sleep as late as we wanted, and we got to watch lots of TV.

When the other kids got back, they would brag about all the stuff they got to do and show off their presents. We would be jealous but act like it was no big deal, like we were not one bit impressed.

I know the houseparents must have dreaded coming back to work after their week off. Things were always chaotic right after Christmas—lots of arguments and fights among us guys. Big surprise. I pretty much stayed on restriction the entire month of January. Being left at the children's home over Christmas week was not a good feeling. But now I wonder if being allowed to leave, then having to come back might have been even worse.

At nine fifteen the next morning, Anna knocked on my door. "Hey, lazybones, you awake?"

"I am now." I was glad I kept my door locked.

"Up. Up. Come on. Breakfast in ten minutes."

I crawled out of bed and pulled on some clothes.

When I crossed through the breezeway, I looked out and saw the two little neighbor boys outside with their dad, riding new bikes. I stood there a minute, watching through the screen. Their mom was out in the driveway, still in her robe, cheering them on, and telling them to make sure they kept on their helmets.

I had not put on a jacket, and it was cold standing there. I hustled on into the kitchen. Nobody was in there, but man, something in the oven smelled good. My stomach growled. The table was set with dishes that had Christmas trees on them. Orange juice was in the glasses. I poured myself a mug of coffee and went into the living room. Christmas music was on the CD player. The only lights were the ones on the tree.

Anna came in from her bedroom. She had on a red sweater with a big reindeer on the front. "There you are. Ho! Ho! Ho! Merry Christmas! Now, where's Mike? Goodness, getting you two up and moving this morning has been like trying to herd chickens. I remember years past when everyone would be up and wanting to open presents at six in the morning."

"Here, Mom." Mike came down the hall. "Merry Christmas." He gave her a hug, then went to the hearth and poked at the fire. "Morning, Josh."

Anna pulled some packages from under the tree. "Breakfast'll be done in a few minutes. You guys open your presents."

She was more excited about the gifts than we were.

Mike and I had identical boxes. Red paper. White ribbon. When I shook the box, nothing rattled. Clothes maybe?

"Go on. Open them."

We pulled off the ribbons and tore off the paper. I lifted the lid of my box and pushed back layers of green tissue paper. It was a sweater. Brown. Heavy. Soft and with a rope pattern knitted in.

Mike opened his box. His was a sweater, too, similar to mine, but his was blue.

"Do you like them?"

"Nice, Mom. Really nice."

"This is great, Anna. Thank you."

"I hope they fit because there's no taking them back if they don't."

Mike held his up. "How come?"

"I made them."

"You did? I didn't know you could make a sweater."

"I've been working on them for months. Started on Josh's in June, yours in October. Try them on. All that work, I'm dying to see how they look on you two."

Mike pulled his sweater over his head.

June. Before I got sick. Back when I was being a jerk. I

was refusing to eat at her table, and Anna was knitting me a sweater.

It did not make any sense. This room. These two people. I didn't deserve any of it.

My sweater fit perfectly. I stood up so Anna could get a good look.

Mike pulled a box from under the tree. "This one's from me. Sorry about the wrapping."

The package was heavy. It had a torn corner, and the bow was coming off. Anna and Mike watched as I ripped into it. Inside the box was a long, black case. "What is it, a clarinet?" I joked.

"Open it." Anna was more excited than Mike, and he had a grin on his face as wide as the moon.

I pulled the case from the box, set it on my knees, and lifted the latches.

Mike was watching my every move.

I lifted the lid and could not believe what I saw.

A telescope. Something I had always wanted. Something I had never dreamed of actually having.

"I don't know what to say. This is great. Man, this is the best. Thank you. Thank you so much! This is awesome!"

"It's not new, but I think it's a good one. I got it from a guy at school."

"It's as good as the ones we used in class." There were not enough telescopes to go around. We had to take turns, and I never felt like I got enough time. Now I could look all I wanted for as long as I wanted.

What an awesome gift—way more than I deserved.

Anna's breakfast casserole was great. After we ate it, we bundled up and went for a walk around the neighborhood. Later we stretched out and watched *A Christmas Story,* one of

Anna's favorite movies. I had never seen it before, but it was really funny.

"Did you have a good day?" Anna asked me that night before I headed back to my room.

"Oh yeah, a very good day. Thanks for everything. I really appreciate it. All of it."

She laid her hand on my arm. "Good. I'm glad. It was a good day for me too. I'm really happy you're here. You know that, don't you?"

I nodded but could not say any more. It had been good. But it was hard too. When you have gone without something all of your life, then you get it in abundance, it can feel like too much. Maybe like sitting down to a huge meal after not having anything to eat for a couple of days.

Sure, it's good, and it fills you up.

But it can make you hurt too.

Eleven

"GREAT NEWS." ANNA pulled a pan of hot rolls from the oven. The pork chops and baked potatoes she placed on the table made my mouth water. I was tired and hungry.

It was the day after Christmas. Mike and I had just come back from the church. A windstorm had come through Christmas night, knocking down dead limbs and branches from the dozen trees surrounding the building. One of the deacons had called Mike early in the morning, looking for volunteers to help clean up. I had gone along with him, figuring they could use an extra set of hands and another strong back.

I was right. We cut limbs and hauled brush, raked, and completed several hours of general cleanup. I spent the better part of the afternoon up on a ladder, cleaning out the gutters.

Mike dropped ice into the glasses. I pulled plates from the cupboard and set them around the table. Anna placed the chops on a platter.

"Lori called. She's coming tomorrow. Going to stay a week."

"Awesome. Guess she's out of school." Mike grabbed spoons from the drawer.

"Who's Lori?"

"My favorite niece," Anna said.

"My favorite cousin," Mike said.

"Lori's great. You'll love her," Anna said. "She's a school-teacher—teaches second grade. We used to be really close. She came up here all the time. But living two hours away and teaching full-time, she can't get away as often. We don't see her nearly enough."

I don't know what I expected—I guess someone old. But when Lori showed up, she did not match what I had in mind. First off, she drove up in an old, restored pickup truck. Second, she was much younger than I thought you had to be to become a teacher.

"I'm twenty-two," she said when I asked her.

Only three years older than me.

"I finished high school a year early and went straight to college." We were playing Scrabble, Mike, Lori, and me. No big surprise, she was beating us badly. Lori was tiny, maybe a hundred pounds, with red hair cut shorter than mine and a nose stud. I usually didn't like nose piercings, but it looked cute on her. She was funny and energetic. She talked enough but not too much. She was one of the nicest girls I had ever met.

Not that I knew much about girls. I never had a girl-friend—not a real one. At the children's home, we would have get-togethers with other cottages, and there was this one girl I talked to. I think she liked me, and I would always be on the lookout for her at church. But then one year, she did not come back from Christmas break. She had gone to her older sister's house for the holidays, and I heard the sister decided to keep her. I was glad for her. Not glad for me.

That night after Anna went to bed, Mike and Lori and I stayed up, shooting the breeze. The two of them went way back. At one time they had lived near each other.

"Those years we lived close, we were more like brother and sister." Lori was putting up the Scrabble board. We carried our soda cans and popcorn bowls to the kitchen. She pushed back the curtains over the kitchen sink to look out the window. "Anybody up for a walk? The moon's full. Not too cold. Who's game?"

"Now?" Mike looked at his watch. "It's after one. Not me. I'm heading to bed."

"I'll go." I pulled on my jacket. "Come on, Mike. Don't be an old man. Sure you don't want to come?"

"Absolutely sure. I'm beat. See you guys in the morning." Mike yawned and headed down the hall to his room.

Lori and I crossed the yard to the street. The air felt cold and crisp. No wind. No clouds. Big white moon and lots of stars in a black sky.

"You're right. It's nice out tonight," I said. I liked looking at the stars even more after taking the astronomy class and using the telescope Mike had given me for Christmas.

"I love walking at night, but it's not safe where I live, like it is here." Lori had her hands shoved deep into the pockets of her jacket.

"Even here, I don't know how safe it would be for a woman to be walking alone at night," I said.

"You're probably right. Thanks for coming with me. After sitting so long, I needed to move."

When we left the house, I thought we would take a quick trek around the block and then come in, but Lori had other ideas.

"Want to walk to the duck pond?"

"The one at the park?" It was a good two miles away, but I wasn't sleepy at all. "Sure."

It was weird out walking the streets in the middle of the

night. We saw only a few cars, but probably half a dozen cats skulking around in the darkness. When we got to the park, Lori sat down on a bench. I followed and sat down next to her. Even though my body was tired, my mind was completely awake. Sitting there on a little hill, we could see the moon reflected in the water a little ways below us.

"See Orion?" I pointed. "And Pegasus?"

"Show me."

"Over there. Look." I pointed out the constellations and described them.

"I think I see them. Cool. How long have you been interested in astronomy?"

"As long as I can remember. I've always loved looking at the sky. It's beautiful. No matter who you are or where you live, whether you're rich or poor, you still get to look up and see the same sky."

As soon as I said that, I wished I hadn't. Guys don't talk like that. I hoped she didn't think I was some emotional freak.

"I never thought of it like that," she said, "but you're right."

I cleared my throat. "Astronomy—it's a hobby, I guess. I've never been big into science in general. Just stars."

"Well, it's an interesting hobby."

"More interesting than video games? That's what normal guys my age are into."

Lori pulled lip balm from her pocket and smeared some on. "I consider normal to be highly overrated."

"You think so?" I teased. "So are you normal? Isn't that a requirement to be a teacher?"

"Absolutely not. Anyone who signs up to teach second grade for what I get paid is definitely not normal. I'd consider it an insult if someone thought I was." She laughed. "I'm sort of kidding. I'm just a regular girl. Working. Trying to make a living and make a difference."

"You like teaching?"

She shrugged. "Been way harder than I thought it would be. The school where I teach has a lot of kids from low-income homes. Lots of single-parent homes. Not exactly *The Cosby Show*, if you know what I mean."

I laughed. "I can definitely relate."

"You grow up with a mom and a dad?"

"Nope. They died when I was little."

"Sorry. Bet that was hard."

"It is what it is." I was ready to talk about something else. She wasn't.

"So who took care of you?"

"Foster parents. Then a children's home."

"Must give you a lot of compassion for what kids go through."

"I guess." I stretched my legs out in front of me. "I don't usually tell people I just met about my past. Ever considered interrogation as a second career?"

"I like hearing people's stories."

"Okay, then. Now it's your turn. What's your story, Miss Lori?"

That was all it took. She talked about graduating from high school a year early and about how difficult it was being a teacher at twenty-two. After all her work and all the money she and her parents had spent on her education, there were days she wasn't sure teaching was what she wanted to do.

"You close to them? To your mom and your dad?"

"To my mom? Yeah. My dad? Not so much."

"That's too bad. How come?"

Lori twisted the silver ring she wore on her thumb. "Long story—not one you want to hear. But no big deal. We get along fine."

Right. I was the master at not telling people my stuff. It didn't take any kind of great skill to see there was something about Lori and her dad she did not want me to know.

But that was cool. Everybody deserves some privacy.

"So," I asked, "which do you like better—cats or dogs?"

"Love dogs. But I have a cat. Easier when you live in an apartment."

"What about music? Country or rap?"

"Neither. Country gives me a headache."

"No way. Me too."

She laughed. "Okay, my turn. Mountains or beach?"

"Never seen either one."

"You're kidding."

"Nope. Which is better?"

"The beach, definitely. But the mountains are nice too."

And so it went. We talked and talked, with none of those awkward gaps, until we both began to yawn. "Ready to head back?"

She nodded. "I think my rear's asleep. I may not be able to stand up."

I held out my hand, and she let me haul her up. Like that was any big deal, considering how tiny she was. We both stretched a bit and headed back the way we had come.

I had left my watch at home, so I was really surprised when we got to the house and found out it was nearly five o'clock. "Good night. I mean, good morning," I said.

"I enjoyed our walk. Thanks for going with me." Lori yawned and leaned against the doorframe. "Later."

"Yep. Later."

ANNA AND I were sitting on the back deck. It was one o'clock in the afternoon, and I was having my first mug of coffee of the day. Man, was it a good thing I had the week off.

That hadn't been my first reaction when I heard the city was going to shut down most operations for two weeks during the holidays. Apparently they did that every year—only kept on a skeleton crew. And no work meant no pay. I had enough money put aside to be okay—barely—but it still made me mad.

Until today.

"So." Anna set down her mug. "You and Lori stayed up awhile last night."

"Yeah, we walked to the park. Got to talking, lost track of time. She up yet?"

"I think so. I heard the shower a little while ago."

"Where's Mike?"

"Gone to the store for me."

Good. There was something I wanted to ask Anna, and I needed privacy to do it. "Want more coffee?" Stalling, I stood up to go refill my cup. When I got back, I handed Anna's mug back to her. "You know that stuff I told you? About the foster home and the fire?"

"Yeah."

"Have you mentioned any of that to Lori?"

"No, it's never come up."

Relief.

"Why do you ask? Are you thinking she should know about it?"

"I guess. I mean, I don't know. Sometime. Of course. I'd like to be the one to tell her is all."

"I understand. And I give you my word I won't mention it. The story is yours to tell whenever you think the time is right."

Anna stood up and stretched. "Thought I'd make pizza for dinner. Lori loves my homemade crust."

"I knew she was a girl with good taste." Anna's pizza was amazing, especially the crust. Who knew you could even make pizza at home?

"Lori has extraordinary taste. And not just in food." Anna raised her eyebrows over her mug.

"What's that supposed to mean?" Like I didn't know.

"Nothing." She shrugged. "Just an observation; that's all."

 Twelve

THE WEEK AFTER Christmas flew by. Mike and Lori and I hung out every day. We went to the movies a couple of afternoons. We went out to dinner. One day we piled into Lori's truck and drove to the house of one of Anna's friends to go fishing in his lake. It was so cold the fish weren't biting, but we had fun anyway. I was hoping for another chance to talk to Lori one-on-one, but it never happened. Whatever Lori and I wanted to do, Mike thought was a good idea too.

On Sunday, the day Lori had to leave, the four of us went to church together. After the service and the coffee hour, we all walked back to the car.

"Do you go to church when you're at home?" I asked Lori. I wondered if she was a regular church kind of girl or if she had gone only today because of Anna and Mike. We had talked a little about God that night on our walk but not at all since then.

"Every Sunday," she said. No surprise. "Bible study on Wednesday evening too," she added. "How about you?"

"Oh, I go sometimes."

Mike had his Bible in his hand. He gave me a look as he opened the car door for Lori.

"Actually, I went some when I was a kid, but then I stopped. I've only been a couple of times lately."

Mike shut Lori's door. She rode in the front with Anna. Mike and I climbed in the back.

We stopped for burgers on the way back to Anna's. Lori was in a hurry to get on the road. Not me. I wished she wasn't leaving at all. I wished the week could go on forever, but tomorrow I would be back at work. In another week Mike would be back in school, and my night classes would start up again.

So much for the holidays. Back to the real world.

Mike and I helped Lori load her stuff. Anna sent her off with a box of her favorite peanut-butter cookies.

"Be safe," Anna told her. "Call. Let us know you made it home."

Lori gave all three of us hugs. We stood in the driveway and watched her drive off. But she hadn't been gone from Anna's an hour before I called her. I just had to hear her voice. "Just checking. Making sure you're doing okay."

She laughed. "I'm still an hour from home, but I think I'm all right. And you—you're still doing okay? Since the last time I saw you, which was—let's see—all of fifty-five minutes ago?"

All right, it was lame for me to call. But I could not stop myself. Not then and not every night over the next two weeks. Every call lasted at least an hour. Lori and I had not been able to talk alone when she was in town. Now that she was at home, we were making up for lost time.

It was Anna who noticed I was going to my room earlier than before. I had told her a couple of times that I was expecting a call. And once Lori had called me while I was helping clean up after dinner. Even though I tried to cover, it was not hard for Anna to figure out what was up.

"So," she said the next evening at dinner, "you and Lori have been talking."

Mike looked up. "On the phone?"

How else? "Couple of times."

"What's up? She tutoring you over the phone?" Mike reached for another spoonful of mashed potatoes.

"Not exactly."

Anna was smiling. Mike was not.

"So why are you calling her? Why's she calling you?" His face said he knew—and he didn't like it.

Mike and I finished the meal without talking to each other. Anna tried to keep up the conversation, but she gave up too. We ate as quickly as possible. Soon as he was finished, Mike put his plate in the sink and told us he had stuff to do. I stayed behind as usual to help Anna in the kitchen.

"Don't take it personally. Mike, I mean." Anna was drying as I washed. "Lori's like a sister to him. He's protective of her."

"Like she needs to be protected from somebody like me?"

"It's not you. He'd be that way about anybody."

Anybody like me.

I ran more hot water.

"I knew you two were hitting it off. I could tell that first night there was an attraction between you."

"I guess Mike didn't catch the same vibe."

"What can I say? A mother—" She caught herself. "I mean, a friend knows these things."

Things?

"Lori's a sweetheart. You're a great guy. I think it's wonderful you two are getting to know each other."

"I'm going to see her this weekend."

Long pause. Did Anna think that was great too?

"It's a two-hour drive."

"Yep. I'm taking a half day off work. Should get to Lori's about the time she's home from school."

"Sounds like a plan. I hope you have a wonderful time."

"Thanks. Should I tell Mike?"

"Nope. Let me."

I do not know what Anna told Mike, but dinnertime was so cold the next night, I wished I had worn a jacket.

"Mike, can you pass me the beans?"

He shoved them my way.

"I hear Dave Matthews's new CD is out." We were both DMB fans. We had talked a couple of times about trying to go to a concert.

No response.

"Today I saw our old road crew cutting and hauling a bunch of that brush away from that bad intersection. You know—the one south of Main."

"I'm so glad," Anna said when Mike didn't give a response. "Should make it a lot safer. Too many bad wrecks there. You couldn't see with all those low-hanging limbs."

Not a word from Mike. Not that night or the next one after that.

After that every little thing I did irritated him. If I set the table and forgot to get him a fork, he took it personally, despite the fact I had also forgotten to get one for myself. When I snagged the newspaper first so I could look at the sports, it ticked him off. Basically, the fact that I was breathing the same air as he was ticked him off.

Anna told me to blow it off, to give him some time. Fine. I hadn't done anything wrong.

At least not where Lori was concerned.

I tried not to let Mike's being mad get to me. But how could it not? The guy was my friend. I had let myself get comfortable in this house with him and Anna. Too comfortable.

Old feelings of insecurity chased me, especially at night. What if Mike decided he wanted me to leave? Anna would have to take his side. He was her son, after all. And what was I? Nobody. Anna had told me the room was mine for as long as I wanted, but I had learned a long time ago that people do not keep their word. I didn't want to leave, but I figured I better come up with plan B, just in case. In the meantime I started watching what I said and what I did as much as I could.

But the thing was, as much as Mike's coldness bothered me, as fearful as I was about doing something wrong and having to leave, none of that was enough to stop me from seeing Lori. I do not think anything could have stopped me. When I thought about her, I could put all the other stuff out of my mind. Nothing else mattered. She was in my head.

Friday afternoon I left work at exactly noon. I rushed home and showered. When Mike drove up a few minutes after me, I was coming out of the house with my duffel bag.

"What are you doing home during the day?" I asked. I hoped he wasn't sick.

"Forgot something. A notebook. Came back to the house to get it."

I figured he was lying, but I let it go.

"So you're going," he said.

I nodded.

"Why are you doing this?"

What a question. "Doing what? I like Lori. She likes me. I want to see her. So I'm going."

"That's it?"

"Well, yeah. What else do you want me to say?" I wavered. Was Mike right? No doubt Lori was out of my league. Who was I to think somebody like her could see anything good in somebody like me? But . . . she had asked me to come; hadn't she? That should count for something.

"Am I interested in your cousin? Yes. Who wouldn't be? Should you be worried I'm going to hurt her or take advantage of her? No. She's a great girl. And no wonder—she comes from a great family. If it wasn't for you and Anna, I wouldn't have met her. You think I'm going to do anything to mess this up? No. I give you my word."

"You're staying the whole weekend?"

"Be back late Sunday."

"Where're you staying?"

So that was it.

"With one of her teacher friends and her husband and kids. They live in the same apartment complex. I'm bunking on their couch."

Mike tried to be cool, but I could see his relief.

"She's like my kid sister."

"She's not a kid."

"And neither are you."

We looked each other in the eye for the longest time. I gave in first and looked at my watch. "Later, man. I got to go."

When I pulled out of the driveway and onto the street, I looked back to see Mike still standing in the street, watching me drive away.

Thirteen

ONCE I MADE it to Lori's town, I followed her directions to her apartment complex. It was nicer than any place I had ever lived, not counting Mike and Anna's house. I parked and walked around the complex until I found her building.

Standing outside her door, I got nervous. What if after all those hours on the phone, we didn't have anything left to talk about? What if after spending the weekend with me, Lori figured out what a loser I was? Worse, what if she decided that tonight?

Honestly, I was so spooked that if Lori had not seen me through the peephole and opened the door, I might have gotten in the car and driven back home without even knocking on the door.

"You made it! Come on in." She grabbed my hand and pulled me inside. "I thought you'd never get here."

Oh man, she looked so good. Those eyes. That smile. Not to mention the rest of her. I would have been content just to sit and look. As for us not having anything to talk about—ha. From the time I walked in, we had to concentrate hard not to talk at the same time. It was crazy.

"What time did you leave?"

"Were your kids good in class today?"

"What did Anna say when you told her you were coming to see me?"

"Are you sure your friends are okay with me staying with them?"

"Do you like ribs? I know this great place."

And then when we both stopped talking long enough to come up for air, Lori took my breath away. We were sitting on the floor, cross-legged, facing each other, playing with her cat. Without warning, she leaned over and kissed me. Quickly. Such a fast kiss that later I wondered if I had imagined it.

"I'm so glad you came."

"I'm so glad I'm here."

The cat padded its way back and forth between us. Its tail swept across my face, and I sneezed. Once, then three times in a row.

"Are you allergic?"

"I don't think so." I sneezed again.

"Maybe you are." She got up to get me a tissue.

What if this was a deal breaker? I had heard about girls and their pets. I had to get this right. "Come here, Max." I scooped him into my lap and began to scratch behind his ears. He purred. And I sneezed again. I spent most of the evening wiping my nose and scratching my eyes and trying to convince Lori all I had was a cold.

But it was so worth it. Every sneeze. Every scratch.

Friday night we hung out until it was time for me to go to her friend's. Later, while propped up on my borrowed couch, I thought about how easy it was being with her. She was so relaxed. So real. Honest. Whatever Lori said, she meant. I can't tell you what a relief that was to me. After what I had been through, I valued people being straight with me more than just about anything else.

I got to her door so early the next morning I had to wait outside while she got dressed. We couldn't stop yawning over the McDonald's breakfast I had bought for us.

She finished her biscuit. "What do you want to do today?"

"Be with you."

"What if I'm doing something awful like emptying the cat box?"

"Long as we're doing it together, it's all good by me."

Max meowed for fresh food.

She giggled. "Good answer, but don't be disappointed. I changed Max's litter before you got here yesterday."

"That's too bad."

She gave me a little punch in the arm. "How about something else? Want to see my school? Want to see my classroom?"

"I'd love to."

"Wow!" Lori's classroom was amazing. "You did all this?" Every wall was covered with art and colorful posters. Cool things hung from the ceiling.

"Oh no," she said. "Lots of it is stuff the kids did."

"I bet your kids love coming in here."

"Not every kid and not every day."

"They love you. I bet they all do."

"I try to love them."

Seeing Lori in her classroom showed me a different part of her. She was responsible for twenty-five kids. For teaching them to read and do math.

"I'm impressed."

Later we went to the park. I bought us hot dogs from two ladies with a cart, and we ate them standing up. Man, were they good.

"Want another?" I asked.

"Do you?"

"I think so."

"I'm so glad because I was dying for another one, and I didn't want you to think I was a pig."

After we ate, Lori pulled a bag of stale bread from her purse. We fed the ducks, then sat on a bench, which reminded us both of that first night when we took our moonlit walk.

That night we tried to watch a movie from Netflix, but we kept pausing it to tell each other something. Finally we gave up and just sat and talked until it was time for me to go back to her friend's apartment.

Sunday morning, we went to Lori's church. She spoke to a lot of people on our way to her favorite pew. We sat down behind a row of her friends, and they turned around to say hello. Everyone was friendly, but it was easy to tell I was being checked out.

The service began with a prayer and then some songs. Lori had a pretty terrible voice, to be honest, but that did not stop her from singing her heart out. I looked over at her once to see that her eyes were closed; she was so into the music. Seeing her like that made me feel like I was witnessing something really private, something between her and God and nobody else. It didn't take me long to look the other way.

After church we went back to Lori's apartment and had lunch. Roast beef from the Crock-Pot, potatoes, salad—all of it good. All I could think about was how much I did not want to leave.

I tried to make conversation. "How'd you learn to cook?"

"My mom. You'll have to meet her."

"And your dad?"

"Sure." She salted her potatoes.

"They must be really proud of you. College graduate. Good job. On your own."

"I guess." She got up to get the pitcher of tea. "I mean, my mom is. Dad's not so easily impressed."

"I bet he is but just doesn't say it."

We finished lunch with a Sara Lee chocolate layer cake. "Sorry. I'm not much of a baker." Lori slid it out of the box.

"Not a baker? You're kidding me?" I pretended to be shocked. "We might have to call this whole relationship thing off right now."

"Stop." Lori laughed. "Really, these cakes are pretty good." She cut us both big corner pieces.

I forked a bite. "Okay, you're right. I suppose I can overlook your one failing."

We chewed in silence for a moment. Finally I got up the nerve to talk to her about something that had been on my mind. "I hope it's okay to ask you this. Just tell me if it's not. I'm sure you've dated a lot of guys. You ever been serious about anyone?"

"Actually, no. In fact I haven't had a boyfriend since I was fifteen."

"How come? I'm sure lots of guys are interested in you."

"Some. I wouldn't say a lot." She fiddled with her napkin. "I've had some guy friends, but not much more than that. What about you?"

I told her about talking to the girl at the children's home, even though it made me sound like a loser. Then I told her I had gone out with a couple of girls, but it had never come to anything much.

"So you've never—?"

I shook my head and avoided her eyes for a second. Was I supposed to be embarrassed? Or proud?

"That's good, Josh," she said slowly. "Really good."

Man, I was relieved. I reached across the table to touch her hand. "So we're in the same place, you and me." I didn't want to come out and say it, but she knew what I meant.

"Yes, of course. Absolutely." She gave me a little sideways smile.

"You realize that makes us abnormal, don't you?"

"Does it?"

"Well, yeah. How many twenty-something-year-old virgins do you know?"

Lori glanced down, then raised her chin to smile right at me. "You're right. Not that many."

Enough serious talk. She began clearing the table. I stood up to help. "So when are you planning a trip to see Anna?"

"Anna?" Lori grinned. "What about you?"

"Okay—and me. When? Next weekend would be good." I would have begged if I thought it would help.

"Can't," she said. "Got stuff going. But maybe in two weeks."

Two weeks. My stomach took a dive. Maybe she wasn't into me the way I was into her. If she was, surely she would not wait that long. When it was time for me to leave, Lori walked me down to my car. We stood there talking, me not wanting to say good-bye, for another forty-five minutes. Finally I couldn't stall any longer.

"I have to go. Really. This time I do."

"I know."

I wanted to kiss her, bad. But I didn't. Except for the little peck she gave me. Not the whole weekend and not then. Next time. Maybe. I so did not want to mess this thing up.

Fourteen

"I'm not making dinner tonight." Anna was sitting at the table, reading a magazine, when Mike and I came into the kitchen after work, neither of us doing much speaking to the other.

"Okay." Mike leaned against the fridge. "You want to go out to eat?"

"I can go pick something up," I said. "Pizza? Burgers? What do you want?" I was okay with her not making dinner. Sometimes we got takeout or made ourselves sandwiches because Anna had somewhere to go.

"I don't want anything."

"Got a meeting?"

"No. I'm staying put. Going to heat myself up a nice can of chicken noodle. It's you two who are leaving."

Mike and I still were not talking to each other any more than was necessary, but we gave each other a look.

"They're needing volunteers at the soup kitchen downtown. It was in yesterday's paper. Said they've been really short on workers lately. There's been a stomach virus going around among the volunteers, and a bunch of them are down for the count this week."

Great. Just what I needed. Another round of throwing up.

"Don't you have to sign up or something?" I heard hope in Mike's voice.

"I think you do." I pretended disappointment.

"Yep. And you did—by proxy. I called up the people and told them to put both your names down. So hop to it, both of you." She looked me over. "Josh, you'd better change clothes. They expect you to be clean and tidy. You're on the late meal sitting. They do two a night. They're expecting you in half an hour."

"I wish you'd said something about this before. I've got a test tomorrow."

"I've got a project due."

Anna turned the page of her magazine. She was not impressed. "Then I guess you'll both be staying up a bit later than usual tonight."

She was not going to move. So we did. I went to my room to change. Then I met Mike in the driveway.

"May as well ride together." I had my keys out.

Mike didn't answer, but he went around and got in.

Neither of us said anything on the way. We were both ticked. Here we were, two grown men, and she was treating us like kids.

Anna was rarely bossy. She treated us as equals. For the most part we operated as three independent adults sharing a house, even if one of us was paying rent. But when Anna took one of her rare stands, neither of us was up to bucking her.

Mike told me where to turn. The soup kitchen was in a part of town where I had never been even though it was close to the motel where I had stayed when I first came to town. If I had known about it back then, there were nights I would have shown up for a free hot meal.

WHERE HURTING ENDS AND LOVE BEGINS

"Man, look at all those little kids." Mike nodded toward the one-story building. It was surrounded by a high chain-link fence. Inside the fence was some playground equipment and about thirty kids running around like it was recess at an elementary school. "I thought it'd be a bunch of old men."

We parked down the block and made our way to the place. When we got there, we told a guy we were first-time volunteers. He opened the gate and showed us which door to go in. It opened right into the kitchen.

"Hey, guys." A big guy with bushy gray hair stuck out his hand. "Here to help out? Appreciate it. I'm Ed. Not sure what you're doing here? No worries. We'll put you two to work." He rocked back and forth while he talked. "Uh-huh, that we will do. First stop, fellows, the hand-washing station. Then Lounelle here will get you your aprons and your hairnets."

Lounelle looked to be about a hundred and fifteen years old. She was obviously thrilled to be assigned to seeing that the likes of us put our hairnets on properly.

Once we were properly humiliated, Mike and I got down to work. First we chopped a bunch of tomatoes for salad. Elbow to elbow. After that we cut pies and put pieces on little individual plates. Then we filled the glasses with ice for tea and lemonade. Mike scooped. I held the cups. Finally we put out forks and napkins, salt and pepper. Spaghetti and meat sauce was on the menu, cherry pie with ice cream for dessert.

When everything was ready and it was time, somebody opened the outside doors and people rushed in. The dining area was one big room with about thirty round tables, each big enough for eight people to sit at. When everybody was seated, Ed gave a short devotional lesson from the book of Psalms. Everyone, even the little kids, stayed quiet when he spoke. Then he said a prayer.

Once he said the amen, it got loud in there. These people were hungry, but you could tell most of them were here for the good time as much as for the food. They were laughing and talking. Kids were goofing around, and their mothers were trying to make them behave. Different groups of people sat at different tables. There were families who sat together— mom, dad, kids, and grandma. Other tables had mostly men. You could tell by their clothes that they had worked all day.

People in the kitchen filled plates and handed them over a counter to those of us doing the serving. As quickly as we could, Mike and I and three other volunteers carried the filled plates to the tables and set them in front of the people I had heard Ed refer to as "our guests." We also served them what they wanted to drink. If anyone needed an extra napkin or dropped a fork, we took care of that too.

It was a good ways from the kitchen to the farthest table, so Mike and I ran our legs off. A couple of guys tried to put one over on us, saying they had not been served when I had seen with my own eyes that they had already eaten full plates. My face got hot, and I started to say something, but Mike stopped me.

"Let it go."

I shot him a look.

"So they want more spaghetti. What's the big deal?"

Not the point. But I did what he asked and moved on to another table where a kid had spilled his milk.

After we had served the last plate, wiped the last table, and swept up the last crumb, we pulled off our hairnets and our aprons and got ready to go. Ed and Lounelle met us at the door.

"You boys saved our hides tonight. Don't know what we'd have done without you. Can you come back again?"

Mike and I looked at each other.

I'd had a good time. The kids were cute. It felt good to do something for somebody else.

"Can I put you down for one night a week? We serve this meal Monday through Thursday."

What did those people eat on the other nights? Boxes of cereal flashed through my mind. My brothers and I with nothing else to eat.

"I need some regulars. People I can count on."

If I'd had time to think, I probably would have come up with some excuse. As it was I couldn't think of a reason to say no. "Sure, I guess I can do that. For one night."

"How 'bout you, son?" Ed knew how to tighten the screws.

"I'm in," said Mike. "At least as long as I'm in town."

"Fine. Fine. We'll look for you then. Next Tuesday night. Drive safe, now."

It was a short drive home, maybe ten minutes. Anna was already in bed when we got home. And we were starving. We had served all that food but not eaten one bite ourselves. Mike got the peanut butter and bread out of the pantry. I went for the jelly and the milk. And for the first time in forever, there was no tension between Mike and me as we shared our meal.

We were cleaning up our sandwich stuff when my cell rang. I looked to see who it was.

"Lori?" Mike asked.

I nodded.

"Better answer it. You know how impatient she gets."

"No problem. I'll call her back." The phone kept ringing in my hand. I fumbled to silence it.

Mike shoved the milk in the fridge. "Later." Then he turned and headed down the hall to his room.

I was seconds away from doing the same when Anna

called my name. She wasn't in bed after all but dozing on the couch within earshot of the kitchen. "Hey," she said, "take it. At least he's talking to you about her. It's a start."

A small one. But yeah, a start.

Fifteen

"So you're coming? This weekend?"

"Be there by eight."

I could hardly wait. Six weeks had passed since the first time Lori and I met. We talked every night. And so far the longest we had gone without seeing each other was two weeks. Even if the weekend got cut short because of something one of us—usually her—had to do, it was worth it to us to be together for even one day. We took turns making the trip.

The past week or so, our conversations had become more serious, something I did not know how to handle. Neither of us came out and said it, but it was pretty obvious we were both thinking of a future with each other. I had started going to church every time Mike and Anna went, even reading my Bible and sometimes saying prayers. It wasn't that I was trying to impress Lori, though that was all right with me too. It was more like I was willing to do whatever I could to become somebody who was good enough for her.

The problem was I couldn't do it. Every time I thought

that maybe Lori was really falling for me, I would remember who I was and what I had done, and I would be ready to pack my car and leave in the night.

I was in a terrible spot. I was falling in love with a perfect girl who did not deserve the likes of me. I couldn't stop myself from doing whatever I could to get her. But at the same time, I knew I didn't deserve what she thought of me.

Mike and Anna and Lori and I shared a late dinner after Lori arrived that Friday. We laughed and joked around, but I could tell something was not right with her. After Mike and Anna went to bed, Lori and I moved to the breezeway, a good place to talk. She was shivering even though it wasn't all that cold. So I went to my room for a blanket.

"Better?" I put it around her shoulders.

"Thanks." She kept shivering.

"Good week at school?"

"It was okay."

"How's ol' Max doing?"

"He's all right."

"Dinner was good."

"Uh-huh."

Trying to keep this conversation going was wearing me out. "Hey, you okay? Tired?" This wasn't Lori. Either she was coming down with something, or she wanted to break up. I'm honest enough to admit I hoped she was getting sick.

"I'm fine," she started to say, but then her voice went away. Her chin went to her chest.

I knelt in front of her. "Hey, something's not right. Talk to me."

Lori was crying. She wouldn't look at me.

I stood up and moved my chair in front of her so we were sitting knee to knee. "What's the matter? Did I say something wrong? Did I do something?" I couldn't think of one thing. Maybe she really was breaking up with me.

She shook her head and kept crying. Finally, she raised her eyes to look at me. "There's something I need to tell you. It's been making me crazy. I decided this weekend I had to get it out in the open."

"Okay, spill it. Whatever it is, it can't be that bad." I tried to hold her hands, but she pulled away and wrapped her arms around herself.

"I'm not the person you think I am. There's something you don't know. Something only a few people know about."

I sat still and waited for whatever was coming next. I was not even a little bit scared. Whatever bad thing she thought she had done, it was going to be no big deal.

"When I was fifteen, I had this boyfriend. He was the same age as me."

"Okay." I knew this already.

"We were stupid. We did things we shouldn't have done." I waited.

"I got pregnant."

"You what?"

No way. I was not hearing this right.

"We hooked up. I got pregnant."

Her words were like a punch to my gut. My hands went cold. "But you said . . ." My mind went back to our conversation of just a few months ago. "You mean you lied to me?"

"I didn't mean to." Lori was crying so hard she could hardly talk. "That conversation—it came out wrong. You thought I was this perfect person. I was afraid you'd be done with me if you knew the truth."

"So you have a kid?" I was stunned.

"No." Her voice was a whisper. "You don't understand.

I was so scared. I didn't know what to do. The night I told my parents, my dad got so mad he couldn't stand to look at me. Even now, he has nothing to say to me. He's never forgiven me. My mom wasn't mad, but she was so hurt. So disappointed. They thought I was their perfect little girl.

"I had this older friend who told me about a clinic. She took me there the next day while my parents were at work. Since I was only fifteen, I was supposed to have to have parental consent, but I used my friend's fake ID.

"They said they wanted to help me and they would take care of everything. I did what they told me to do. When I came back the next day, I put down on the paper that I was eighteen."

I swallowed. "What kind of a clinic was it?"

She looked at me as if she couldn't believe I was asking her that. "Josh, please. You know. Don't make me say it."

"You had an abortion."

She nodded. "I don't know what I was thinking. I guess I just wanted it all to go away. But of course when my parents found out, the situation got worse. My dad called me a murderer. My mom cried for a month."

I couldn't look at Lori, couldn't think of anything to say. I felt like a fool.

All my life, people had fed me bull. And all I wanted in the world was someone I could trust. Someone who would be straight with me. I had thought Lori was that person, but now . . .

I just couldn't believe it. The thing that mattered most was now shattered.

"Josh, say something." She put her hands on mine.

I pulled away. "What do you want me to say?"

"That you understand. That you don't think I'm a terrible

person. Tell me that you're not going to write me off like my dad did. Anything. Just say something. Please."

"Understand? Give me a break." I could feel my face getting hot. "What I don't understand is how you could have lied to me. What did I ever say to make you think I'd be mad if you'd been with a guy?" I was yelling now. "You're a beautiful girl. Honestly, I was surprised when you told me you were a virgin. It wouldn't have mattered to me if you'd been with somebody. You should've known that. I didn't expect you to be perfect, but you had no reason to lie."

"Josh, please. Let me explain."

I didn't give her a chance. "There's no explaining. You got pregnant. You had an abortion. Okay. What else have you lied about? What's the next thing you're going to tell me that's not true?"

"There isn't anything else. I promise. You can trust me."

I stared at Lori, but I did not see her.

Yeah, right. Trust. What a joke.

I had trusted the policeman when he told me everything was going to be all right. I had trusted my foster parents when they let us believe we were wanted and safe. At the children's home I had trusted my houseparents when they told me that someday the right adoptive parents would come along for me.

"I did trust you. I thought you were different. I believed you were the one person I could count on to be straight with me."

"I am that person. Believe me. I didn't mean to hurt you. I didn't mean to tell you something that wasn't true. That's not who I am."

"Then why did you lie?"

She swallowed. "I didn't exactly."

"Come on."

"I was afraid you'd never want to see me again. Just like my dad."

I stood up. "I guess it turns out you were right, but not for the reason you thought. You could have told me anything, and I would have been okay with it."

She met my eyes.

"As long as it was the truth."

I didn't see Lori the rest of the weekend. I stayed in my room mostly. When I left to go get something to eat, I went out through my door to the outside. I didn't know what she told Mike and Anna. I didn't care. She could figure it out.

When I got up early Sunday morning, her car was gone. Mike knocked on my door later to see if I was going to church. I told him no. I didn't see any need.

Lori tried over and over again to call me, but I didn't answer. She left me voice messages, begging me to please talk to her. She said she did not want to lose me and that I was the best thing that had ever happened to her.

For a while I had let myself believe the good thing we had was real. I had been stupid to think I could actually make a go of things with her. I had been ready to plan for a life together, but now? No way. I wanted no part of Lori. No part at all.

After a couple of weeks she quit trying to reach me. Which was fine by me.

At least that's what I told myself.

 Sixteen

ANNA TRIED TO talk to me about what was going on, but I shut her out. I shut everybody out. I was mad at Lori, mad at myself, and mad at the world.

Every little thing bugged me. I got so ticked off when my cell phone quit that I threw it across the yard. I know. Real smart. At least I took my anger out on an object instead of a person, which I've done too many times.

All I could think about was how nothing good had ever happened to me, and nothing good ever would. And no wonder, I thought. People get what they deserve—nothing more, nothing less.

But then we got the news about Mike.

And I realized how untrue that was.

He went for his regular checkup, the one he had to go to every six months. When I got home from work, I found him sitting outside on the deck.

"Wanna shoot some hoops?" I had forgotten he had an appointment even though we had talked about it at dinner last night.

He shook his head. "Maybe later. Probably not. I don't know."

I was headed to my room, but the strain in his voice made me stop. I turned around, climbed the steps to the porch, and sat down next to him.

"Saw my oncologist today." Mike pulled a leaf from a bush and started picking bits off it, letting them fall to the ground.

"Everything okay?"

"Nope, it's not."

"Something wrong? It was just a checkup, right? Routine?"

"I've had thirteen good appointments. Thirteen appointments when the doctor said the scans were all clear and he'd see me in six months." He looked off in the distance.

I waited.

"But that's not the news I got today."

"What, then? What did the doc say?"

"The cancer's back."

I sucked in a breath. "Man. Are they sure? I've heard about doctors making mistakes."

"No mistake."

"But they can take care of it, right? You'll be okay. You fought it once; you can fight it again. Right, man? Piece of cake. So what do they do? Chemo? Radiation?"

Mike looked sideways at me, like I was crazy or something. No wonder. I was such an idiot. Trying to sound like I had a clue what I was talking about, which I obviously did not.

"I don't know what they're going to make me do. Last time it was chemo. I have to go back tomorrow to find out the plan."

"Have you told Anna?"

"Not yet. Haven't gotten up the nerve to go inside. She doesn't even know I'm home yet." He sighed and shook his head. "I hate this. Not just for me. For her. I mean, things are finally going good. She's happy. There haven't been many bumps in the road lately. And now this."

"Hey, it's not like you're sick on purpose. This is not your fault. But you've got to tell her. She'll stand by you. I will too. I can take you to the doctor or the hospital, whatever you need. I'll help Anna. It'll be all right."

I looked over at Mike. He was staring down at the ground as if he hadn't even heard me. "Maybe it won't be that bad this time around," I said. "Was it that bad before?"

Mike wiped at his eyes with the back of his hand. "Pretty bad."

I sat there on the porch with Mike until he got up the courage to go inside and talk to his mom. I figured they would want some privacy, so I went to my room. I wasn't sure I should come to dinner or even if there would be any dinner, which was no big deal because I wasn't hungry. I lay on my bed and stared at the crack in the ceiling. All I could think of was what a good guy Mike was and how he didn't deserve to be sick.

Sure, we had our issues—actually, only one issue, and we had settled that one. The only time I saw Mike show his backside was over me and Lori. And looking back on that situation, I don't blame him.

Back when we were both on the work crew, everybody liked Mike. Even though he was a college guy and most members of the crew would never make anything more of themselves than what they were, he had treated everyone as equals. So instead of resenting him, the working guys had asked him about his classes and told him to study hard. They had claimed Mike's success as if he was one of their nephews.

The thing was, Mike cared about people. He put himself out there. And people responded to that. He made a difference with people.

I'm not proud to admit this, but after going to the soup

kitchen a half dozen times, I had had enough. It was hard work, hot back in the kitchen, and the whole thing got to me after a while.

"This is getting to be a drag," I told Mike on the way home from serving one night. I was tired of wiping off greasy tables, and I was mad that most of the time nobody even acted like they appreciated what we were doing. "They have plenty of help lately. Nobody will even notice if I don't show up. And I've got better things to do with my time."

Mike actually got hacked off at me then. "What's the matter with you? Of course they'll notice. Those little kids are all over you from the minute we show up. It wouldn't be right to quit. Besides, what's the big deal? We go down there once a week, three hours tops. It's important. Suck it up, man."

Even if I didn't like it, I couldn't figure out a good argument. So week after week we showed up. And it turned out Mike was right. I always felt better about myself and my life after going and serving food to those people, especially the little kids. Truth is, they kind of reminded me of myself back in the day.

So I owed that to Mike—that he kept me going when I wanted to quit. Actually, when I thought of it, I owed almost everything I had to him. Sure, I had found my way to town, but he had helped me find my way for real. He was the reason I had a place to live and was going to school. And he could have resented sharing his mom with me, been jealous of the time and attention she gave me. But no, he included me in his family, treated me like a brother, and didn't mind when his mother treated me like a son.

I owed him big for that.

I did not pray on a regular basis. I wasn't even sure I believed in prayer. But lying there on my bed, I sent one up for Mike. I asked God please to take care of him. To take care of all of us because we were really in need of whatever he could do.

I'm not sure how long I lay there, but I jumped when somebody knocked.

"Josh, dinner's ready. You coming?" Mike was outside my door.

"How'd it go?" I asked him while we were still in the breezeway. "Did she take it okay?"

Mike shook his head, so I expected to see Anna all upset. But when I got to the table, it was like dinner as usual. Weird. Anna moved around the kitchen and set out taco meat, shells, lettuce, tomatoes, cheese, and salsa. Mike put ice in the glasses. I set out plates and forks.

We sat down, put our napkins in our laps, and bowed our heads for Anna to say the blessing like she did every night.

"Dear God, we thank you for this day and for this . . ."

But then she couldn't finish. I looked up and saw her shoulders shaking. She put her hand to her mouth.

Mike did not look up. He kept his head down and finished the prayer. ". . . food. We are thankful for all your good gifts. We ask your blessing on us now as we eat. Amen."

Then we sat there until Anna got herself together.

"Mom, it's going to be okay."

She nodded. Then she got up, got a tissue, and blew her nose. "Sour cream. I forgot sour cream. Mike, you like sour cream on your tacos, and I forgot to buy any." Her crumpled face said that Mike having sour cream was the most important thing in the whole world to her.

"No prob." I jumped up. "Won't take me a minute. I'll go get some."

Anna stared at me.

"Josh, no. I'm fine. We don't need sour cream. Come on and sit down. Let's eat."

But I was already gone.

I HAD NEVER been around anybody who was bad sick. Not like this. Starting the very next day, Mike had one appointment after the other. It was unbelievable how they got everything set up so fast. Usually it takes two weeks to get a doctor to look at your toe. I was afraid this meant the doctors were scared there wasn't much time.

And there were a lot of doctors. Mike had to see his regular oncologist, the special radiation oncologist, an internist, even a surgeon. He had appointments with a nutritionist and went in for lab work and x-rays and other scans. Our little town did not have all the stuff Mike needed, but there was a big hospital with good doctors only half an hour away. That was where he had been treated before and where he would go back.

Mike only had a couple of months left until graduation. Two days into all this and after all those appointments had been set up, he got the bright idea that he would talk to the doctors about holding off on his treatment. He explained his reasons to me. "I'm so close, and it's taken me so long to get this far. Last time knocked me down so low I had to drop out. I don't want to blow it now."

I was driving him to appointment number two. He had convinced Anna that it was embarrassing for her to go with him every time. "Are you crazy?" I said. "This is your life you're talking about." I was mad at him for even thinking about waiting on treatment. "Forget college. You can do that later."

"Later is right." He stared out the window. "I'm twenty-seven years old, living with my mother. If I hadn't gotten cancer in the first place, I'd be long gone by now." He turned back to me, his face intense. "You don't know what it's like, feeling like everyone else has left you behind. Like there's something wrong with you. Like you'll never get what you want. I feel like one of those dogs chasing after the fake rabbit. No matter how hard I try, it's still out of reach."

Mike never talked like that. He was Mr. Positive, encouraging everybody else and always seeing the good in people and situations. Sometimes he got on my nerves, looking on the bright side of everything. I had never known him to feel sorry for himself.

"Hey, man, it's tough, I know. Sometimes life kicks your butt." I did know those feelings. Not what it was like to have cancer. But everything else—I was right there. Mike could feel sorry for himself all he wanted. Cancer twice before you're thirty earns you that.

MIKE HAD BEEN to the oncologist's office. He slammed the kitchen door on his way in. I looked up from the sandwich I was making. "Are they going to let you wait on starting treatment?"

"Nope. Nixed that idea before I could even explain why I wanted to. The doctor said we've got to get on this thing ASAP. Like yesterday."

"We'll get through this." I grabbed two Cokes from the fridge. "You're not alone. I'm with you every step. We've had our differences, but through this we're tight, man."

Mike gave me a look.

"I know. You don't have to say it. I can be a jerk sometimes, but hey, so can you."

He popped the top on his can, turned it up, and took a big swig. "That's a really nice thing to say to a dying man."

Was he kidding? I couldn't tell.

"Stop. Don't talk like that. Nobody said you were dying. I'm serious. All that stuff about Lori—it's over and done with. No hard feelings? I need to know. We good?"

He finally smiled. "We're good."

"All right then."

"All right then. Now give me half your sandwich."

"No way." I whirled around, barely missing his grab at my plate. "Get out of here. Make your own."

"And I thought you were my friend."

Despite the kidding around, I knew Mike was bummed. Was it because he might not finish the semester or because he understood how bad things were?

I'm not sure he knew.

Seventeen

MIKE GOT PUT on the prayer list of every single church in town. A bunch out of town too. Somebody put up a website so people could keep up with how he was doing. The site had a map of the world on it where you could see where people were praying for him. It was crazy how the news spread and how more and more people seemed to hear about it. People who did not even know Mike, even people in other states. Then it jumped to people in other countries.

Mike needed every prayer he could get. Because even though his doctors insisted he start his treatments right away, he was determined to get his degree anyway.

At first he did really well. They gave him some steroids, which pumped him up, made him hungry, and gave him energy. He felt good enough to go to class. Sometimes he had to miss because of appointments, but his professors worked with him, and he was able to keep up with his work. My community college basics were nothing compared to Mike's last semester as an engineering major. There were tons of projects and papers he had to finish up, as if his professors were trying to cram everything they had forgotten to teach into these last couple of months. Every evening he worked on getting as much as he could finished ahead of time.

The doctors decided Mike had to have chemo and radiation. Hitting the cancer from both sides, I guess.

They started with the radiation. He had to go five days a week. The treatments were not too bad at first. Mike drove himself. He felt more tired than normal, and he got this rash, like a sunburn, but he said it didn't hurt all that bad. Even with the steroids, he wasn't hungry. Anna made him chocolate milkshakes with peanut butter and protein powder every night. And not just the milkshakes, but anything else she thought he would like. Fried chicken, homemade pizza, pasta with meatballs and garlic bread dripping with butter—you name it, she made it for Mike.

He lost twenty pounds. I gained five.

Then the chemo started. They gave him medicine to prevent nausea, but he still threw up. He lost his hair and so much more weight that he looked like one of those prisoners you see in old war movies. He could walk but not far at one time without nearly falling over.

But Mike was stubborn. Even feeling that rotten, he tried to go to class. I didn't get it, but he was so determined. Because he was dizzy sometimes, the doctors wouldn't let him drive. So every day he had class, Anna dropped him off and picked him up even when he had late classes. Some mornings from the kitchen we could hear him throwing up. Then in a couple of minutes, he would come to the refrigerator, grab a Sprite, act as though everything was great, and be ready to go.

I had just gotten home from work on a Friday evening when Anna came and knocked on my door.

"What's up?" I could see on her face that something wasn't right.

"It's Mike. He's in the ER."

"What happened?" I was already putting my shoes back on.

"I don't know. They wouldn't tell me anything. Just said I needed to come."

We were out the door.

When Anna and I got to the hospital, Mike was not happy. "No big deal. I was at the soda machine and got a little dizzy. Somebody panicked and called 911. I was fine. All I needed to do was sit down a minute. But no, they called EMS, loaded me on a stretcher, and brought me here in an ambulance."

No big deal.

Right.

Mike had six stitches in his head where he had gashed it open when he fell. And his blood count was so low that they would not let him go until he got a transfusion. The docs wanted to admit him for a couple of days, but he talked them out of that. So they did everything in the ER. By the time we got home, it was three o'clock in the morning.

The next day, Anna and I were eating eggs at noon. When Mike got up, he came into the kitchen and sat down with us. Except for the gash in his head, he actually looked better. Not so pale.

"Want some breakfast?"

"Maybe later."

"Sleep well after your wild night? I know I did." Anna got up to get him some juice.

"I slept okay."

"How many more weeks of school?" I asked.

"I don't know. Doesn't matter. I'm done."

"What do you mean?"

"I can't do it anymore. I thought I could make it until the

end, but I can't." His shoulders slumped. His voice was flat. "No big deal. It is what it is."

I had thought he was crazy for trying to finish, but hearing him give up scared me. What if this meant he was tired of fighting the cancer? What if he was ready to give up on all of it?

"Could you make it in a wheelchair?"

"I don't know."

"I bet you could."

"We can call today and get you one." Anna set his juice down on the table. "You can try it out this weekend. Next week, on campus, we'll be ready. I'll push you anywhere you need to go."

I saw the look in Mike's eyes. No guy likes the idea of his mother taking care of him like that. It would be embarrassing, and having cancer was embarrassing enough. He was bald and so thin and pale. I saw how people stared at him now.

"I know you would, Mom," he said. "I appreciate it, but I don't know if it's worth it. Let me think about it over the weekend." He shifted his hips in the chair and closed his eyes for a second. "I could use a pain pill. If it's time."

She got up to get the pill, a glass of water too.

While she was gone, I moved closer so I could speak low. "Let's get the wheelchair. I've got a little time off built up at work, and I bet they'll work with me on my schedule. Things are slow right now anyway. So I'll help you out until you get stronger. I can go with you to class, take you wherever you need to go."

Anna came back with the pill. She heard what I said. "What are you talking about? I can help Mike. You don't need to miss work."

Mike got up to go to the bathroom.

"I want to do this for him. It'll be good for him. For me too."

Anna resisted, but eventually she let me win. She understood, but it was still hard for her. When somebody you love is sick, you want to do something. Anything. And it stinks when there is really nothing you can do to make things better. No matter how many meals you cook or miles you push a wheelchair, that person is still sick and suffering.

When things are like that, doing the right thing can take all the strength you have.

UNTIL YOU EITHER ride in a wheelchair or push one for somebody else, you can't fully appreciate things like handicapped parking places, sidewalk ramps, and elevators in tall buildings. Getting Mike where he needed to go was a bigger job than I had expected.

Not that I'm complaining.

I'm not complaining about helping him out of the car, which got easier in one way because he kept losing weight but harder in other ways because he was so weak he couldn't always help very much. Or about toting his backpack of heavy books, his medicine, and his little oxygen tank.

I'm not complaining about the times I raced down a hall, hoping no able-bodied person was in the handicapped stall so I could hold Mike up while he vomited into the toilet.

That he let me do all these things, for me, was a gift. I know—sounds cheesy, even to me. But it was the truth. Like a hidden birthmark, my guilt over the fire was with me every day. But the guilt and my lifelong loneliness and feelings of isolation were lessened by being able to take care of Mike and help him out. I don't understand it, but I know that's how it was.

I guess that means my motives weren't pure. That I was selfish, getting something out of taking care of a sick person. The good thing is that Mike didn't know that. Or maybe he did, but he didn't care. He just wanted to go to class. Simple as that. And so we did.

They cut me a lot of slack at work. Some days I went in at noon, some days not at all. I only put in my full eight hours on days when Mike didn't have a class, but I squeezed in some extra on the weekends when they could use me. My boss told me not to worry about it, to do what I had to do.

So that's what our days were like. Chemo. Medicine. Class. Repeat.

Then came finals and final presentations—an extra crazy time.

And then, finally, graduation day.

I don't know how Mike did it. Sheer will is all. Well, that and God. If God cares anything about people with cancer getting their engineering degrees, that would mean he had a part in it too.

Mike never asked, "Why me?"—at least not where I could hear it. He didn't talk about how it stunk to be twenty-seven years old and have the body of an old man. He didn't talk about what would happen if he didn't get better.

Did he think about it? I know I did. I thought about it all the time. The doctors had given Mike the odds on whether he would beat the cancer or not—30 percent chance he would make it, 70 percent he wouldn't. I had thought they would do tests all along to see how things were going, but I was wrong. There would be no testing until his treatment was finished the second week of June.

Wouldn't you know? It rained on graduation day. Mike weighed about a hundred and ten by then, and his skin was a gray color. He had a sore on his hind end from sitting on it so much since he could not walk anymore. But he was happy. Man, was he happy. He was smiling when I helped him out of bed, smiling when I helped him shave and dress in his cap and gown, smiling and whistling "Pomp and Circumstance" when I wheeled him down the hall from his room and into the living room.

When we made our grand entrance into the living room, we were greeted by applause from Anna and from Lori, who had just arrived. I knew she was coming to see Mike graduate, but I didn't realize she had arrived while I was helping Mike get ready.

Seeing her was like a punch in the gut. It had been almost three months since our breakup. Felt like two days. She had on this white dress that showed off the tan she had gotten riding her bike to school every day. Her hair was longer and blonde instead of red. But her smile was the same.

She rushed over to Mike to give him a hug. When she raised up, I was still standing behind Mike's wheelchair, so we were eye to eye.

"Hi, Josh"—like nothing was wrong.

"Hey, good to see you. Glad you came." I didn't know if I was lying or telling the truth.

"Couldn't miss this big event. No way."

Then it got awkward. But Anna stepped in.

"Pictures. Time for pictures." She fiddled with her camera. "I hate that it's raining. I wanted to take them outside. Let's do it in front of the fireplace."

I positioned Mike's chair just the way she wanted it, then reached to take the camera from her. "I'll take the pictures. Get in there next to Mike."

I took pictures of Mike and his mom, of Mike and Lori,

of the three of them together, then of Mike by himself. "It's a wrap," I said when I had snapped them all. I looked at the mantel clock. "And just in time. Mike and I have to get going. We're supposed to be there early."

"Wait." Anna moved toward me. "I want pictures of you and Mike."

"No, you don't." I wasn't family. They didn't need to be looking at these pictures years from now and have to wonder, who was that strange guy next to Mike?

"Excuse me, but I absolutely do want some of you. Now, stop stalling and get over there next to the graduate." Anna snatched the camera from my hands and motioned me toward Mike.

He grinned at me. "Come on. You know better than to argue. You're never gonna win."

So I knelt down beside my friend. He put his arm on my shoulder, and we smiled for the camera just like we had been told.

MIKE FELT OKAY for about a week after graduation. He was even able to go out with Anna and me to celebrate my twentieth birthday, a little late. But then everything went downhill. Mike came down with pneumonia and had to go to the hospital for five days. While he was there, I went back to work so I could save as much time off as I could.

Working gave me a break from everything, but it did not take my mind off anything. I did not think Mike was doing good. He slept most of the time, and he had a hard time eating because of blisters in his mouth from the chemo.

Lori had gone home to finish out her school year, but as soon as school was out for her, she came back to help.

Having her around was awkward and tense at times, but we handled it by treating each other real politely and never ending up alone together in the same room. Besides, having somebody in the house whose life was on the line put things in perspective. Our last words to each other had been bad, but without spelling it out, we sort of managed to put our personal junk aside.

Actually, I was grateful to Lori for being there. Anna was so focused on Mike that she let stuff go. It was like nothing else existed outside of his meals, his treatments, and his medicine. She lost weight herself and sometimes wore the same clothes three days in a row. One night I came home from work and there wasn't any electricity—she had forgotten to pay the bill. Somebody needed to step in and look after her. Lori saw what was going on and, without me having to say anything, she took on that job.

I had my hands full with Mike. After he came home from the hospital, he was really weak. He could not go to the bathroom by himself, and he did not want Anna helping him. We talked about it, and I ended up moving into his bedroom. So anytime Mike needed to go in the night, I was right there beside him.

He hated needing help. I know he did. Sometimes he would try to get up without waking me. I usually woke up anyway, but I would pretend I was asleep, just waiting in case he needed me.

Then one night he fell. I heard him hit the floor and jumped out of bed, wide awake.

"You okay?" I helped him get up off the floor. He had wet on himself, and I had to help him get cleaned up.

"I'm all right. I'm sorry." He was sitting on the toilet.

"It's okay. No big deal." I tossed his wet pajamas into the corner of the bathroom.

"You think you broke anything? Did you hit your head?"

"No. I didn't fall hard—just slid down. I'm all right."

Once I got Mike back to bed, I lay down on the cot I had set up next to him. I could tell by his breathing that he was not asleep.

"I need to ask you something," he finally said.

"What? You need a pain pill?"

"No. I'm not hurting. I need to ask you something."

"Okay."

"Something happens to me, I don't make it, would you look after Mom?"

"Don't say that. Nothing's going to happen to you. You're going to beat this thing."

"Josh, I'm tired. Really tired."

Tears came in my eyes. I couldn't think of anything to say. I just nodded in the darkness.

"I don't know what's going to happen," he went on. "I want to make sure Mom's all right. It's been just me and her so long, she's gonna take it hard. But you get her. You know how to talk to her. She loves you."

I loved her, too, but I couldn't say it. "You don't have anything to worry about, man. You're going to be fine. But sure, I'll look out for Anna until you're back on your feet. Count on it."

"Thanks. That's all I need to know."

 Eighteen

MIKE DIED IN his sleep that night. He took his last breath with me asleep next to him.

I couldn't believe it. I still can't. I should have been pre-pared, but it felt so unexpected. He hadn't even been back for his scans to see if the treatments had worked. Sure, he had gotten weaker and thinner, but none of us dreamed he was that bad off.

I heard that sometimes it is the chemo that kills you, not the cancer. The doctors wouldn't say, but I don't think they were as surprised at what happened as we were. Looking back, I can see that the signs were there and we chose not to see them. We wanted Mike to keep on fighting. We truly believed he would win.

All those prayers—what is a person to make of those? In the days after Mike's death, people talked a lot about that. Some people said God answers every prayer, but sometimes his answer is no. Some said that God loves us and he gives us strength. Some said he suffered with us while we were suffering.

Honestly, I didn't understand much of what people said. But something was happening to me. I had started praying for Mike, mostly because everyone else was, and it seemed like something I should do. And when Mike died, I just sort of kept on praying. Maybe it was just a habit by then. But I would tell God what was going on, even when the only thing going on was that I was sad and mad.

But the thing is it helped.

At least most days.

Anna took it hard. And no wonder. One day she was looking at the calendar to see when her son's next doctor's visit was, and the next one she was having to pick what funeral home to use. How do you decide something like that? She looked ten years older in one day. Lori did not leave her side.

People from the church came by. You have never seen so many loaves of banana bread. People tried to help, but there wasn't much anybody could do. Anna couldn't sleep. Wouldn't eat. And she cried off and on all the time. "Just give me time," she kept saying. "I need time."

Time did help. A few weeks after Mike's death, Anna was doing some better, getting up and getting dressed every day and at least eating breakfast most days. There were still tons of details to take care of—thank-you notes to write, legal papers to be filled out, and such. Most of that fell on Lori's shoulders. Lori also began helping Anna go through Mike's things. Anna wasn't ready to get rid of anything, but she was up to doing some sorting. Mike had a lot of stuff, so it was a big job.

I was back at work by then. My spare time was spent maintaining the house and the yard, looking after Anna's car—doing anything I could think of to help.

It wasn't like Anna was elderly or in terrible health. But she was so alone. No husband. No children. She was an only child, and her parents were dead. Lori's dad and Mike's dad were brothers, so she was actually only a niece by marriage.

WHERE HURTING ENDS AND LOVE BEGINS

Like me, Anna had no blood relatives to stand by her. So Lori and I sort of became her family.

I can say that for two people who had hurt each other so badly, Lori and I did an amazing job working together. We already had seen each other's worst selves. Taking care of Mike and now Anna, we were reminded of each other's best selves.

Three weeks after the funeral, Lori and I sat together on the back deck. Anna was inside taking a much-needed nap. Lori stretched her feet out in front of her and sipped on a Sprite. "Have you thought about what you're going to do now?" she asked me. "Will you stay here now that Mike's gone?"

"Absolutely. I promised him I would."

"What do you mean? When did you promise him that?"

"The night he died. It was like he knew or something. He asked me to take care of Anna if something happened to him. I blew him off, told him he was going to be fine, but he wouldn't let it go. So of course I promised him I'd look out for her."

"Forever?"

"Looks like it. I'll be here as long as she needs me."

"That's taking on a lot. What about when she gets older? You know, when she can't take care of herself?"

"She's a long way from that."

"But one day it will happen."

"I don't know how it will all work out. One day at a time, I guess. I'll do the best I can."

Lori set her Sprite down and leaned back on her hands. "You're a pretty amazing guy."

"Mike's the one who was amazing. Not me."

Lori blinked back tears. "He was like a brother to me. I miss him so much. Every morning since he died, I wake up and think it can't possibly be real. I think, *Surely he's still here.*"

I should have taken her hand then, but I didn't. I missed Mike too. The year I had spent living in this house with him and Anna had been the closest thing to having a real family I had ever experienced. Simple things like hanging out at the dinner table and shooting hoops in the driveway had meant so much. Watching how he and his mom loved and respected each other had taught me how to do the same.

When Mike died, it felt like there was this big hole in my life. The house felt empty without him. Even though he had been a fairly quiet guy, the silence of him being gone was louder than any voice I had ever heard. I would walk into the kitchen and feel this enormous thing in the room. Except it wasn't a big something. It was a big nothing.

Lori pulled a Kleenex out of her pocket and blew her nose. "I love Anna, but it's not going to be the same coming here for visits now that Mike is gone."

"You're right."

"It's not going to be the same for you, being here without Mike either."

I knew that too. I did not want Anna to think I was trying to take Mike's place. And I did not know if I should tell her what Mike had asked me to do or not. That had been weighing heavy on my mind the past few weeks. Did she have a right to know? Would it make her feel better or worse?

"I'm going home Friday," Lori said.

"Does Anna know?"

"I told her. Will you be okay without me here to help out?"

"I'll make it."

Lori pulled her feet up so that her knees were under her chin. "It's going to be hard for me to leave. For a lot of reasons." She paused. "There's no chance for us; is there, Josh."

It was a statement, not a question. But I answered her anyway. "Can't go back. It doesn't work like that."

ANNA HAD BEGUN to act a little more like herself before Lori left. Once she was gone, she continued to feel better. I think maybe Lori's leaving was a sign to Anna that it was time to wake up and get back to life.

We had a decent weekend. On Saturday we went to the cemetery. On Sunday we went to church. That was hard. Couple of the songs got to her. She wanted to leave early, so we eased out before the last prayer.

"People mean well," she told me on the walk to the car, "but sometimes they can say the most hurtful things. If I hear from one more person that God took Mike because he needed another singer in the angel choir, I think I might scream."

I nodded. "Anybody who'd say that obviously never heard Mike sing."

Anna stopped and gave me a look.

Uh-oh. It had just popped out. "I'm sorry. I shouldn't have said that. I didn't mean it, really."

She shot me the funniest look. "Oh, Josh, you are so right." She started laughing. "That boy took after me—couldn't carry a tune in a suitcase. Do you know that in middle school choir, Mike was so bad that the director asked him to be the mascot? The mascot! Have you ever heard of a choir mascot? They had never had one before, and I don't think they've had one since." She laughed so hard her face turned red, and she started to cough. "No way Mike is in any angel choir. No way."

By the time we got to the car, we were both laughing. By the time we got home, we were crying. Over the next few days that's how it went. We would laugh awhile and then cry awhile.

I don't know which did more good, the laughter or the tears. What I do know is that we both started feeling better.

We talked about Mike all the time.

Anna told me story after story about what Mike had been like as a little boy. Occasionally she would start a story, but she would stop herself, take a minute, then tell something different. Maybe it was a memory too painful to talk about or, perhaps, too precious. Whatever it was, it was her business. I just listened.

"I've decided to finish going through Mike's room today," Anna told me one Saturday morning two months after his death. "I'll take most of it to Goodwill. Is there anything you want?"

I wasn't sure what to say. Mike was six inches taller than me, but I was twenty pounds heavier than his healthy weight. No way would his clothes fit me. But I did want something of his to remember him by. "You want me to help you? I'll let you know if I see anything I'd like."

It took us all day, but at the end of it we had ten bags and four boxes packed and ready to be donated. I loaded his textbooks in my trunk to take to the used bookstore. Anna kept his Bible and some of his papers. I took a couple of his baseball caps. Lori had asked for his blue-jean jacket and a poster he had up on the wall, so we set those things aside for her. Anna wasn't sure what to do with his high school athletic trophies. I suggested we put them in the attic for storage. She thought that was a good idea.

She also gave me Mike's laptop. I told her I would take it to a computer repair shop and have all of Mike's data removed, but she told me that wasn't necessary. His bank accounts had been closed, his credit cards too. "You took care of Mike," she told me. "I think I can trust you to take care of his computer. The password to get on is *engineermike*."

When we finished packing up everything, I helped Anna move the furniture around. It was a good-sized room. She put a new bedspread on the bed and hung a couple of new pictures on the wall. Mike's closet, once overflowing with stuff, was now empty, except for a few boxes on a high shelf.

"Are you planning on renting Mike's room out?"

"Maybe."

"That'd be good. It'd bring in some cash."

"I've been thinking that maybe you'd like to move into here. We could rent out your old space."

"You mean me take Mike's old room?" I remembered Mike asking me to look after his mom. Was this what he had in mind? I would be closer to Anna in case she needed anything—down the hall instead of across the breezeway.

"It's just a thought." Anna turned her back to me.

"No, it's a great idea. I'd like this room. It's a great room."

"It doesn't have its own bath. You'll have to use the one across the hall."

"No problem."

Anna turned to face me. "Josh, you don't have to worry. I'm not expecting you to fill the void left by Mike. No one can do that. I will always miss him. I'll always have an empty space in my life where he is supposed to be."

I nodded.

"But I am lonely, and I like having you here. You're a good person. You took care of Mike. You're taking care of me. I know you won't be here forever. Big things are ahead for you. But in the meantime, I'd love to have you closer. But if you don't want to give up your privacy, I understand. It was a thought; that's all."

"I'll start moving my stuff over in the morning."

Anna reached out to pat my arm, then gave me a hug

instead. "That sounds great." She teared up a bit. "You are such a comfort to me. I can't imagine what it would be like if I was alone in this house."

I HAD NEVER used Mike's computer much even though he had offered. When I needed one for school, I went to the library. So it felt weird to me to log on with his password, my fingers punching the same keys his fingers had touched. When the screen came up, I didn't see anything out of the ordinary on his desktop. Just the usual—music, photos, documents for school. Fooling around, I clicked onto the Internet to check a couple of my favorite sports news sites, looked at the next day's weather forecast, and played a game of solitaire. Then I downloaded his schoolwork and other files to floppy disks to make more room on the hard drive. It would be great having a computer of my own—make things a lot easier for school. I knew I needed to get one but hadn't been ready to spend the cash.

After a while I decided to look at Mike's photos. The first folder I opened was a group of pics of me and him and Lori taken in December when Lori and I had first met. There were some good ones of Lori, of Mike too. We had passed the camera around. Could it really have been less than a year ago that Mike was so alive? So happy? Looking at those photos, you never in a million years would guess what was ahead.

I studied my own face in a picture Mike had taken of me alone. If you did not know me, would you ever guess my past? How can people look so normal on the outside when we are such messes on the inside?

I closed that folder and opened another. Mike with his mom. Mike with friends at a baseball game. Mike with some random dog. Anna sitting on the picnic table. Pictures of the house, of Anna's flower bed, of Mike holding a basketball.

I lost track of time as I opened folder after folder. Mike must have scanned in all his family's old photos because there were tons of them, the most recent ones first. I saw Mike in high school and middle school. There were vacation photos of him, Anna, and his dad.

I had always wondered why there were not any family pictures in Anna's house. Now I knew. Some people keep their photos in albums, I guess, but apparently Mike preferred a digital record.

When I got to Mike's elementary years, I decided to skip all the way back to the beginning. I was hoping there would be some of his mom and dad when they were first married, and I wanted to see Mike's baby pictures.

I found what I was looking for. His parents looked so young. Anna's hair was blonde instead of gray, and she was thin. Mike must have been born soon after they married because there were not many of just the two of them. I saw Mike as a baby and then as a toddler. There were lots of repeats, and some of the pictures had faded before he scanned them, which was too bad.

There are no pictures of my family that I know of. I only have a few that were taken after my brothers and I went into foster care. So going through those years of Mike and Anna's family photos was like looking at travel pictures from another country. That was what normal family life looked like to me.

Poring over those pictures, I think I was searching for clues. How does a person create a family—a real one? Living with Anna and Mike had shown me a lot, but we were all adults. What would it be like to be a little kid in a real family?

What had it been like for Mike? If I had a son someday, would I know how to give him what I never had?

When I had sat with the computer on my lap long enough for my legs to go to sleep, I knew it was time to shut it down. I had been sitting there for more than two hours. But I opened one last folder that showed the family on an Easter Sunday. Mike in a little blue suit and short pants, holding a basket of eggs, squinting into the sun. Something was different about these pictures, though. Not only did I see Mike, Anna, and his dad, but there was a baby girl with them too. At first I thought it might be Lori, but the eyes were so different I did not think it was her.

I scrolled to find an individual shot of the little girl. She was cute. About three or four. I stared at her pictures for a long time. Something about her made me keep looking. I went back to earlier pictures, searching for group pictures of Mike and his family. She was there. In every shot.

And then she wasn't.

Best I could tell, Mike had a sister, which was a total shock. I found her baby pictures and lots of other shots of her. Something about her looked familiar. She looked a little like Mike.

I tried to figure it out. What had happened to that little girl? Why hadn't Mike or Anna ever mentioned her? I tried to figure it out. Maybe she had been a foster child they had gotten at birth. But if they had kept her so long, why didn't they keep her forever? Nothing I could come up with made any sense.

Finally I couldn't stay awake any longer. I logged off and crawled into bed, thinking about Mike and wishing he was still here.

 # Nineteen

WHEN ANNA CAME into the kitchen the next morning, I was waiting for her.

"You're up early for a Saturday. Want some French toast?" She was groping around, barely awake.

"Sure. If you're making some for yourself." Most week-days I had Pop-Tarts. Not healthy, I know, but I never get tired of them.

Anna started coffee. Got out the milk and the eggs. "Sleep well?"

"Okay." I got out two plates and two forks. This was weird. "Can I ask you something?"

"Sure. What?"

I held two spoons in my hand. "Did Mike have a sister?"

Anna closed the bread bag and secured it with the twist tie. She put the lid back on the coffee can and set it back up on the shelf. Then she went to the sink, where she washed and dried her hands. Finally she came to the table. Her knee grazed mine when she sat down.

"How did you figure that out?"

I got the feeling something wasn't right. "Last night. When

I was messing around on the computer, I saw some family pictures. There was this little girl in every shot up until a certain point, but then there weren't any more of her. I never knew there was another child in the family. Mike never mentioned her. I've never heard you talk about her. I know it's none of my business, but did something happen to her?"

"She passed away when she was six, almost seven." Anna pushed her hair back from her face.

There were a lot of things about this family I did not know. "Did she have cancer? Like Mike?" How awful to lose both your kids. Your husband too.

"No." Anna spoke slowly. "She didn't."

"We talk about Mike all the time. You've told me about your husband. Why don't you talk about your daughter?"

She thought for a minute. "Lots of reasons, really. When Mike and I moved here with his dad, we wanted a fresh start. When Jody died, we were living in a small community. Everyone knew us. Everywhere we went—the post office, the grocery store, church, Mike's school—everyone knew about Jody and how she died. It was difficult for all of us. Especially for Mike. Once we moved here, we tried to move forward. We never forgot her, but over time we didn't talk about her as much. Very few people here know what our family's been through."

That made sense. Sort of. But it didn't make sense to me that she and Mike never even *mentioned* a sister. "I've never seen any pictures of her."

"I have some. In my bedroom. That's where most of the family photos are."

I had never been in Anna's bedroom. Never had the need. Still, I had the feeling there was something she was not telling me. Something she wasn't being straight with me about.

"This may be too personal, but can I ask you how she died?"

Anna picked up an Equal packet and began moving it between her fingers. "An accident."

"You mean a car wreck?"

"No." She tapped the packet on the table.

"What happened then?"

Anna set the packet down. "She died in a fire. It'll be fourteen years ago."

Fourteen years? My stomach dropped.

"She was playing at a neighbor's house when it happened. A little boy, one of her good friends, was playing with matches. It was an accident. He didn't mean to do it."

I stared at her. This was unreal.

Anna placed her hand over mine. Her voice shook. "Her name was Jody. Back then we called her J.J. because when Mike was little, he couldn't say his *d*'s."

J.J. That was her name. I had blocked it out. Now everything came back. Her name. Her face. The girl in the family pictures. I could smell smoke and see flames. I could hear the sirens and shouting adults.

I pulled away from Anna, got up, paced the length of the kitchen twice, then slammed my fist into the back door. The pain in my knuckles was nothing compared to the pain inside my head.

"How could you not tell me? All this time? How long have you known it was me who killed your little girl?" My back was against the outside kitchen door. "You let me live with you all this time, knowing?" I fumbled for the doorknob. "I shouldn't be here. You shouldn't have ever had to see my face."

Anna put her hand on my arm. "I should have told you before now," she said. "I'm sorry. I could never find the right time."

"Did Mike know?"

"Yes."

"How long?"

"We knew right after you moved in. He figured it out first."

I lost it then. I slid down onto the floor and covered my head with my arms.

Anna sat down beside me. "Josh, listen to me. When we found out, I admit, I was shocked beyond imagination. Mike and I both were. Neither one of us could believe it was you. What were the chances of you ending up in this town, much less in our house? We talked about it for days, trying to figure out what to do. We decided not to tell you. That's why you never heard about Jody. It wasn't your fault. It never was. I knew that, and Mike knew that. We had a choice. We chose to be a part of your life. And for you to be a part of ours."

I could not stop shaking and crying. Why hadn't I figured it out? Mike was one of the kids from across the creek. Mike and J.J. I remembered it now. But he looked so different. Maybe the cancer. Or maybe just growing up. But if I had been too stupid to figure it out, how could they have known and not told me?

All that time, he knew. Why? It wasn't right. Me being here wasn't right. If they hadn't wanted to tell me, why hadn't they made up some reason to kick me out?

"Josh," Anna said quietly. "We made the right choice."

No way. What a sick joke. I refused to look at her.

"I forgave you a long time ago. And I'll say this as many times as it takes for you to believe it. You were a child. It was an accident. You are a good person with a wonderful future ahead of you. You may not want to talk to me right now, but I am in your life forever. We are connected. Yes, by a terrible event, but also by love. I will never give up on you."

I wiped my nose on the sleeve of my shirt. "I'm sorry. I'm so sorry. I don't know what to do. I don't know what to say. I'm sorry. I'm really sorry." I don't know how many times I said it. My mind was racing. I stood up. "I'm leaving. I've got to get out of here."

"I wish you wouldn't."

"I shouldn't be here."

Anna held on to the edge of the cabinet. She winced as she pulled herself up. "Okay. If you have to. I understand. Take some time, as much time as you need. But promise me you'll come back. This is your home. When you're ready, we'll talk, and I'll tell you anything you want to know. All right?"

She looked at me, but I didn't answer. I couldn't. When she continued, it was almost like she was talking to herself. "Mike and I had planned on telling you all along. A couple of times we slipped up and mentioned Jody, but each time it seemed that something caused you to miss it. We were waiting for the right time. When he got sick, that time never came."

That really got to me. Anna had lost everything—her daughter, her husband, and now her son. It wasn't right. None of it. Looking at her, all I could see was my part in her grief. I met her eyes for only a second. I couldn't take it. I turned and left out the kitchen door. I crossed the breezeway, went to my room and changed my shirt, threw some stuff into my backpack, and hurried outside to my car.

I drove and drove, up one street and down another until I must have driven nearly every street in town. How had I gotten myself into such a mess? Of all the towns in the state, I ended up here. Of all the jobs, I ended up working with Mike. Of all the places to stay, I ended up in the home of the family whose lives I had wrecked.

Why?

This time when I got to the edge of town, I kept going. I turned onto the highway and headed east. I wanted to talk to Lori. If she would talk to me. She knew this family. Maybe she could give me some answers.

Driving, there was no escape from my thoughts. I pictured Anna as a young mother of two little kids. She washed their faces and made them dinner. She made them brush their teeth and tucked them into bed at night. I saw them all—a husband and a wife. A little girl and a little boy. The perfect family.

Until I came along.

What had Anna been doing when they came to her house and told her that her little girl had died? Had she fainted or gotten sick to her stomach? No doubt she cried.

And Mike—what had it been like for him? He had been protective of his sister. I could remember that. But he hadn't been protective enough. He'd let her play with me. What had it been like to have a sister for six years and then one day become an only child?

I didn't ever meet Mike's dad. If he was any kind of a man, he must have wanted to kill me when he found out.

Too bad he didn't.

Lori and Mike had been close growing up. Did she know I was the one who had killed her cousin? Had she always known and just hidden this from me? Was this one more thing she had lied to me about?

I had to find out.

I took the highway exit that led to Lori's town. After parking and sitting in my car for I don't know how long, I climbed the steps to her apartment and stood outside her door. I hadn't called to tell her I was on my way. That seemed stupid now. I wanted to leave, but there were questions I wanted answered.

I knocked on the door.

"Josh?" She was still in her robe. "What are you doing here?"

"I need to talk to you."

"What's wrong? Is something wrong with Anna?"

"No, she's fine."

"You came all this way to talk to me? Why didn't you call?" It wasn't like she was being cold, more like she couldn't figure out what was going on. Like I had caught her off guard.

"It's important. Please."

"Okay, give me a minute." She closed the door.

I stood outside and waited till she came back. She had put on some jeans and a shirt.

"Can I come in?"

"Of course. Are you okay? You want some coffee?"

When I shook my head, Lori sat down on one end of the couch. I took the other. After driving two hours to talk to her, I could not find words.

"Mike. What is it?"

"I found out something. A secret."

"Secrets can hurt." She looked me straight in the eye.

"Mike had a sister," I said.

"Yeah. He did. Jody died when she was six years old."

"Mike and Anna never talked about her."

She nodded. "Anna asked me not to mention her in front of you or Mike. I argued with her because I thought she was trying to forget Jody. It didn't seem right that she would ask me to do that. She wouldn't explain, but she also wouldn't budge until I gave her my word. I've honored her wishes. But I didn't understand or agree with it then, and I still don't."

"Do you remember what happened?"

"Of course. There was an accident. A house fire. It was terrible. I remember going to her funeral. All the adults were crying. I'd never been to a funeral before, and I was shocked that they'd put J.J. in a box. I didn't know they put people in coffins. Mike's mom and dad stood looking at her for a long time before they let them close the lid." Lori swiped at a tear that had slid down her face. "It's not right what happened. Not right what all Anna's been through. No mother should lose both her children. I don't know how she stands it."

We sat in silence. I could hear somebody bouncing a basketball on the sidewalk outside. I could smell the lotion Lori always wore.

Finally Lori spoke. "You came all this way to talk to me about Mike's little sister. About Anna's child who died fourteen years ago. Why?"

I swallowed. "I have to tell you something."

She waited.

"There's a reason they never talked about J.J. around me. A reason Anna asked you not to mention her name."

"I don't understand."

"What do you know about the fire?"

"Not a lot. I heard it started under the house. That nobody knew J.J. was inside the house and that they found her upstairs. I heard she died from the smoke."

"That's all?"

"Pretty much."

"Did you ever hear how the fire started?"

"No. I figured nobody knew."

"Mike and Anna knew."

"Okay."

"And I know."

"Anna told you?"

"She didn't have to. I was there when it happened. I lived in that house. The people who owned it were my foster parents."

"No way."

"I didn't know anything about the connection until today."

"You saw the fire?"

"I started it."

"What?"

"I was playing under the porch that day. With matches."

Lori had been sitting on the edge of the couch. When she heard my words, she leaned back against the deep cushions.

I shook my head. "It was all my fault. So many things are my fault. I killed an innocent little girl. I destroyed a family's home. I think about what I did every day. If I could go back and change what happened, I would. Knowing what I did is bad. Knowing that I did it to Anna and Mike and his dad makes it worse. I wish it had been me who died instead of her."

Lori got up. She went to stare out the window. "This is unreal."

"No it's real. Too real."

"And Anna and Mike knew all this time who you were."

"Anna said they figured it out right after I moved into the house."

"And they never said anything. They never let on."

"No. They should have told me. I never would've stayed there if I'd known. How could Anna and Mike have lied to me like that? They shouldn't have had to see me every day. They shouldn't have had to see me at all."

Lori whirled around. I was still sitting on the couch. She stood over me. "You don't get it at all. Anna isn't like other people you've known. Mike was different too. I know them. They chose to love you, even knowing what you did. They chose to forgive you. They put everything they were feeling aside for you—not because they were playing you, but because they believed in you. There was a reason they didn't tell you: they love you. They want you to have a good life. Anna will do anything to support you. If Mike was still here, he would do the same."

I had a hard time buying it. "They should've told me they knew. I should've had a choice."

"And what choice would you have made if you'd known back then?"

"I would have left."

"And look at what you would have missed."

I thought of Mike. Of Anna. Of all they had given me.

"You have a choice now," Lori said.

"I don't deserve all they've done for me."

"No, you don't." She sat back down on the couch. "Thankfully, we don't always get what we deserve."

"What about you? She was your cousin. Your friend. How can you stand to be in the same room with me?"

"Josh, what can I possibly say to you?" Her voice broke. "You didn't mean to do it. You were a little guy yourself. I don't blame you—not at all. And how could I? Look at me. You caused a child's death by accident. I caused my own baby's death. And that was no accident."

"I would give anything to take back what I did. To erase that day in my life," I said.

"And so would I."

When I looked over at Lori, it hit me what I'd done. When she was honest and finally told me her truth, I rejected her. But all the while, I had been hiding from her what I had done. Now, after learning the truth about me, she accepted and forgave. I was ashamed.

I scooted closer to her on the couch. "You made a mistake," I said. "You're not a bad person. You were fifteen."

"I knew what I was doing."

Lori was crying now. Not quiet little tears, but big sobs that made her shake and struggle to catch her breath.

So much pain. So much loss.

I pulled her into my arms and held her against my chest. I didn't know what to say, so I didn't say anything until she slowly became quiet. For more than an hour, I didn't move my arms from around her, and she didn't pull away.

I spent that night in Lori's apartment. I know—not a good idea. But we talked until four in the morning about everything. About how I had acted when she first told me about her abortion. She not being straight with me and how that was related to her fear of my rejection of her, the way her dad had. We both said we were sorry about a million times. We worked out a lot of things, set a lot of things straight. When she went to bed, I didn't have the strength to get up and find somewhere else to stay, so I crashed right there on the couch.

The next morning when Lori woke up and came into the living room, I rolled over and saw her face. Even after only four hours of sleep, she was beautiful. That's when it hit me. I wanted to wake up to Lori's face every day for the rest of my life.

I sat up and put my feet on the floor. "You up for a drive?"

"Where to?"

"Anna's. Will you come with me?"

"You've decided to go back?"

"I have."

"Good choice."

And it was.

Ten years have passed since Lori and I made that drive. Eight months after that day, we were married in Anna's backyard. People said we were too young and it was too fast, but we've made it work. Sure, there have been rough spots, but everyone has those. You get through them.

Lori is still not as close to her parents as she would like. But over the years, I have seen signs of them softening up. I tell her not to lose hope, that anything can happen. So she sends them cards and pictures. Sometimes they call. Unfortunately, they live several states away, so we don't get to see them very often. Maybe someday they will move close.

Right after we were married, Lori got a nearby teaching job, and Anna offered to let us stay in her house. She had just been diagnosed with MS, and the doctors told her it wouldn't be long before she would need some help. So Lori and I took her up on the offer, and it worked out well for all of us.

Anna insisted on moving into my old bedroom so we could have privacy. I think she liked it out there—gave her some privacy too. Lots of nights she and I sat together in the breezeway. We talked about Mike, and she told me stories about Jody. Over time, I got to the place where I could remember my past without so much pain. Anna helped me see more of the good in what had happened to me.

A couple of years after Lori and I married, I started nursing school. Taking care of Mike had planted the seed for me to have a career in health care. I've had my RN license for two years now. We're not rich, but I make a decent living for us.

Anna is actually the one who talked me into considering nursing. That woman orchestrated so many good things in my life. Caring for her was something I wanted to do. As far as I know, she never wavered in her belief that I had a bright future ahead. I know she never wavered in her support to make it real.

One afternoon after Lori and I had been married for about a year, I got home from work to see two strange cars in the driveway. When I went into the house, it was empty. Then Anna came in through the back door that opened out onto the deck.

"Come out here, Josh. There're some people who want to see you." She was trying not to give anything away, but I don't think I have ever seen her smile so big.

I stepped outside to a small crowd of folks—two couples and their kids.

My brothers. Sam and Matt. And their families.

You've never seen anything like the hugging and crying that went on. Anna had done the search and set the whole thing up. We spent the afternoon remembering our childhoods and catching up on our adulthoods. I am so thankful that my brothers' lives turned out good. When they asked how things had been for me, I looked over and caught Anna's eye. I could honestly tell them I had been through some rough patches, but it had worked out in the end.

Lori and I have two kids now, the oldest a son. Before he was born, we tossed around a few different names. We even checked out a book from the library to help us decide. But in the end we both agreed there was no choice. His name is Michael. Our boy is too young to understand now, but when he gets older, I will tell him about the man he was named after, the best friend I ever had.

Someday we will tell our daughter about who she was named for too. Our little girl is named Jody Ann.

Not having a father growing up, I've had so much to learn about being a dad. Lori is patient with me. She encourages me when I get it right, and she calls me out when I'm being harsh. Our church offers parenting classes and support groups for dads. I started out taking the classes. The last time they offered a class, they asked me to help lead.

Anna passed away a year and a half ago. I miss her every day. She saved my life. Without her, I can't imagine where I would be and what I'd be without.

We still live in the same house and town where I met Mike and Anna. It is a great house and a great town, a wonderful place to raise a family and to make a good life. When I look back at the twists and turns of my early years, I realize landing here was the best thing that ever happened to me. I am more grateful than I can say.

These days whenever I'm asked to fill out a form or give someone my personal information, I pause at the place where I'm supposed to put down or tell my address.

You see, they haven't officially changed the name of where we live.

But I have.

No matter my real address, my heart knows this one true thing. Because of the choices of two people I will never forget, I will forever and always make my home in a special place.

A place called Blessing.

It is where I live and what I hope to be.

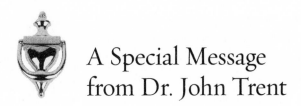

A Special Message from Dr. John Trent

I HOPE READING this story has touched your heart—as writing it has touched mine. Please know that many of the themes you read about in this book are echoes of experiences I have personally struggled with or benefited from. For example, I spent much of my early life wondering if the hurt I had caused others disqualified me from a special future. And it was in the home much like Anna's that I, like Josh, first saw what could happen when a family chooses to give what the Bible calls a blessing.

Of course, at the time I did not have a word for what I longed for so deeply and was so grateful to receive from a loving family. Only later did I come to understand that the Barram family (in my case) were people who chose to employ this incredibly powerful tool for communicating unconditional love and experiencing God's love.

My friend Gary Smalley and I explored the idea of the blessing more than two decades ago in a book called *The Blessing*. Since then more than one million families have learned to follow this simple, profound path to affirming and encouraging others. The results in the lives of individuals and families have been astonishing.

But what is the blessing? It is something we are called to live out as followers of Jesus (Gen. 12:2; 1 Peter 3:9) and especially as parents. It involves looking for specific ways to move toward others and provide them with five essential elements:

- Meaningful touch
- A spoken message
- Attaching high value
- Picturing a special future
- An active commitment

Think back now, as you've finished this story, about when Josh showed up in Anna's home (and for a brief time in the foster home before the fire). From the beginning Anna and Mike looked for ways to give these five elements of the blessing to a hurting young man, and doing so changed all their lives. The same was true in my life story.

The blessing is something everyone longs for in life. Its absence can leave a painful legacy of hurt and rejection while its presence instills confidence and comfort and can even turn a life around. In essence the choice to give the blessing to another person is really a choice to be a conduit of God's blessing.

If you're intrigued by this idea of blessing and want to dig a little deeper, let me make a few suggestions.

First, you can take your reading experience to another level by working through the questions at the end of this book. They are designed to take you back through the chapters, explore the meaning of the story, and tap into your own memories, emotions, and issues. Whether you choose to work through these questions by yourself, in a small group, with a few good friends, or with your spouse, I hope they will challenge and encourage you and help you see more clearly the incredible impact of God's blessing poured through a family. (Special thanks to Kari Trent—whom, with her younger sister, Laura, it has been our honor to parent—for working with Annette Smith and me to develop the questions.)

Second, if you're a book person—which might be safe to say since you are reading this book—I hope you will also consider reading two others that I have just revised and updated. Both are published by Thomas Nelson and can be found in our online store at www.TheBlessing.com.

The first book is *The Blessing*, which I mentioned earlier. This Gold Medallion–award winner examines in more detail the five elements of the blessing. Understanding them can help you see why Josh's life was changed by a family and how you and your family can become an incredible light for others. That book also is the foundation for a seven-year national campaign we have undertaken with Focus on the Family, Thomas Nelson Publishers, StrongFamilies.com, and Barclay College. Our goal, through the relaunch of *The Blessing* and the publication of *A Place Called Blessing*, is for one million parents to give one million children their blessing—to help them thrive today and gain a special future tomorrow.

The second book I want to recommend is my children's book *I'd Choose You!* Beautifully illustrated by award-winning artist Judy Love, it offers a fun, touching, encouraging way for you to teach your loved ones about the blessing. It is a keepsake book as well, with a special section designed to help you write a personalized blessing for your child. Once inscribed with your personal blessing, the book could well turn out to be a lifelong treasure for someone you love. Many of the parents who choose to be a part of our one-million-parents challenge will be using the book to help them capture their written blessing to their children and then keeping the book as a special remembrance.

Finally, we would like to invite you to visit us at our website, www.TheBlessing.com. Look for a red door, just like the one on the cover of this book. Click on this door to take a virtual step into *A Place Called Blessing*. There you will find posts by people who have read the book as well as articles and videos from me and from Dr. Tony Wheeler, the executive director of the Institute for the Blessing at Barclay College. You will also find links, tools, and how to become part of our one-million-parents challenge. You will even find online courses (both certificate training and those offering college, master's, and even doctoral credit) designed to help you, your family, and your church understand what the blessing is and how to live it out more fully here on earth.

If you are like Josh or Lori or me and you have struggled with feeling that some aspects of your past disqualify you from experiencing God's best, look for a section behind the red door on the website called "Reversing the Curse." There you will find help and hope specifically aimed at helping you move away from the hurt of the past and toward God's best today.

Whatever you choose to do next, may the Lord bless your thoughts, your interaction with others, and the next steps that he points you toward as you learn more about living out the blessing. And in the process, may the Lord also put on your mind and heart someone you know who needs the message of this book.

Someone who could use a loving, affirming touch and

words that open up to him or her a special future. Someone you can bless by showing the way to *A Place Called Blessing.*

May the Lord bless and encourage you each day to live out the blessing. And may those God puts in your life story find, in your love, a *person* called Blessing.

—JOHN TRENT

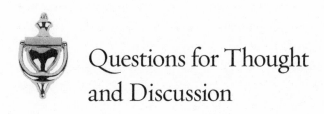

Questions for Thought and Discussion

ONE

1. Learning to trust is one of the first developmental tasks a child must accomplish. How does an infant learn to trust? How do kids learn to trust? How do adults? Do trust issues change as people get older?

2. What basic necessities did the parents of Josh, the young boy of the story, fail to provide? How did this failure influence his ability to trust and color the way he sees the world? In what ways was Josh fundamentally changed by his early childhood experiences?

3. Did you learn to trust as a child? If so, how? If not, what kept you from learning to trust? If you did not learn trust from your parents, did you learn it from someone else? Who? How did he or she teach you?

Two

1. Josh says he did not care about anything as long as he could be with his brothers. Imagine how his separation from them affected him. What was the hardest aspect of this separation for him to deal with? Have you ever been separated from family or friends for an extended period of time? How did you cope with it?

2. Josh is very matter-of-fact in his description of going to a new foster home. What coping skills had he developed during his time in foster care? Were these skills healthy? Think of a difficult aspect of your childhood. Did you learn healthy or unhealthy coping skills (or perhaps a mixture of the two)? Do you still rely on any of those skills today?

3. Josh did not seem to miss his parents or even have feelings for them. Why do you think this is? Have you ever experienced a situation so difficult that you stopped feeling the associated pain? Did the pain ever return? If so, how have you coped?

Three

1. While in the foster home in the country, Josh experienced the most contented feelings of his life. What was so special about this situation? Have you ever experienced similar feelings of contentment? When? Did those feelings last? Do you ever feel that contentment as an adult? What prompts those feelings?

2. Josh states that while he felt safe and cared for in the country home, he did not feel loved. Do you think his foster parents loved him? If you believe so, why didn't Josh feel it? How could they have ensured that Josh felt their love?

3. Josh describes a real camaraderie between himself and the

little girl he played with. They enjoyed sharing secrets. Unfortunately one of their secrets, the candle and matches, had a tragic result. Think of a time when you shared a secret with someone. What was the outcome?

4. When Josh realized the fire was out of control, he could have alerted his foster mom. Why didn't he do that? How might the outcome have changed if he had gone for help? Have you ever hidden from a situation, allowing it to get worse, rather than seeking help? What was the result?

FOUR

1. In this chapter, we see the theme of rejection being played out again and again in Josh's life. First his foster parents rejected him. Then he was left behind by his brothers when their adoptive family did not want him. Later a couple changed their minds about possibly adopting him. How did these episodes of rejection affect the way Josh saw himself—and how he behaved? What coping skills did he develop? Think of a time when you felt rejected. How did you cope? Were your coping methods effective?

2. One of the most heartbreaking scenes in the story was when Josh's brother told him he was going to be left behind while the older brothers were being adopted. How do you think the brother felt about being adopted? Do you think Josh was angry at his brothers for leaving him behind? Have you ever felt abandoned by your family or by your friends? Describe your emotions when that happened.

3. Josh was not the only child not adopted. He describes other boys in his cottage who were never chosen. All of them had some attributes that labeled them as undesirable. How does our society treat those who are less than perfect—physically, mentally, or socially? How do

you as an individual treat those who are seemingly "less than"? Have you ever felt like an outcast yourself? What made you feel that way?

4. Why did Josh want to leave the children's home behind, and why didn't he take advantage of the aftercare program that could have helped him adjust to life outside? What were Josh's three desires once he left the orphanage? How did his past affect his goals?

FIVE

1. Josh found himself homeless after leaving the children's home. Did he fit the stereotype of a homeless person? Was he to blame for his situation? Have you ever known someone who was homeless? What would you have done differently in Josh's situation?

2. What were Josh's expectations when he went to check out the job with the city? Was he confident? When he learned he would need boots for the job, was his reaction appropriate? How close do you think he was to walking out of the interview? Why?

3. Why did Mike reach out to Josh? Why was Josh so reluctant to open up to anyone about himself?

4. Josh was embarrassed at his lack of money. Have you ever been embarrassed by a lack of money, social standing, or education? How did you react to those around you who had more than you?

5. Anna obviously wanted to help Josh, yet she tried to let him maintain his dignity. Was she successful? Have you ever reached out to someone in need? What was that person's reaction? How did this reaction make you feel?

Six

1. Why did Josh feel out of place at Anna's table? Have you felt uncomfortable in someone's home? Why? How did you react?

2. Do you think Anna's relationship with Mike is typical of a mother and her grown son? How does it differ from your young-adult relationship with your parents (or parent)? Did you (or do you) wish for a closer relationship with them? Why?

3. Why did Anna's efforts to get Josh to open up backfire? What could she have done differently? Have your efforts at reaching out to someone ever been rebuffed? If so, how did it make you feel?

4. What do you think of Josh's taking his food to his room?

5. If you were Anna or Mike, would you have stopped trying to reach out to Josh? Why or why not? How do you think Christians should handle this type of situation?

Seven

1. Anna stepped in to help Josh, seemingly with no thought as to whether he would welcome her help. Have you ever been in a place that was so difficult you welcomed all offers of help? If so, how did that experience change you?

2. What do you think about Josh's allowing Anna to pay for his medical care even though he had the money to do so? Do you think Anna knew he could have paid her back? Why did she insist that he "pay it forward" rather than pay her back?

3. Josh's illness was a turning point in his relationship with Anna and Mike. What was it about the experience that changed Josh so profoundly? What would have happened if he had not gotten sick?

EIGHT

1. Contrast the way Mike and Anna cared for Josh during his illness with the way his parents cared for him when he was little. Were your basic needs met by your parents? If not, how does that affect you today? If you have experienced healing from your past, as Josh did, who or what prompted that healing?

2. While living with Mike and Anna, Josh began to see himself differently. What did Mike and Anna do that prompted this change of perspective? Is there someone in your life who does not see himself as worthy or valuable? How can you help them see themselves differently?

3. When Josh was talking with Anna about his past, she spoke words of affirmation to him. How did he react? How do you react when someone points out your best traits? Why is this element of the blessing so powerful? (See "A Special Message from Dr. John Trent" beginning on page 159 for an explanation of the elements of the blessing.)

4. After Josh opened up to Anna about his past, her questions about his brothers caused him to react with anger. Why did he become so upset? Did Anna push him too hard?

5. After Josh confessed his role in the little girl's death, Anna placed her hands on his shoulders. Later she took both his hands in hers. Why did she do this? What did her touch convey to Josh? Why is appropriate meaningful touch a powerful and important aspect of the blessing?

NINE

1. Josh had never considered college. Why? How did Anna change his mind about the possibility?

2. When Josh got called into his boss's office, he expected one thing and experienced something very different.

What happened? Contrast Josh's feelings about himself before he went into the office with how he felt about himself when he left.

3. Why was cutting the Christmas tree so important to Mike? Why was it so important to Anna that Josh go with her to church? What did she hope would happen as a result?

4. Josh had a physical reaction to the candles in the church. Has something ever triggered a memory so strong that you had a physical reaction? Was it a good memory or an unpleasant one? Describe the experience.

5. What led to Josh's feeling that there might be a glimmer of light inside him?

TEN

1. After everything they had done for him, Josh was still surprised that Anna and Mike wanted to spend Christmas with him. Why? What message did his gifts from Mike and Anna convey about their feelings for him?

2. Have you ever been lonely at Christmas? Have you ever done something special for someone at the holidays? Have you ever invited a nonfamily member to spend Christmas day with you and your family? Why or why not?

3. What does Josh mean when he says, "It can feel like too much"?

ELEVEN

1. Before Lori arrived, Josh had not had a close relationship with a woman. What are some of the reasons for this?

2. Josh and Lori had very different backgrounds. Why do you think they hit it off together so quickly?

3. Anna was quick to notice Josh and Lori's attraction to

each other. Do you think she approved? What were her concerns about the two of them becoming romantically involved?

4. Do you think that people who come from broken homes or a past like Josh's can "reverse the curse" and have happy, healthy families and relationships? Why or why not? Can the blessing play a part in this type of transformation?

TWELVE

1. Josh stretched the truth when Lori asked him about his church attendance. Do you think he had given much thought to faith at this point in his life? Why or why not? How did his earlier experiences influence his attitude?

2. Josh was surprised by Mike's disapproval of his relationship with Lori. Was Mike justified in his reaction? What does it say about how he felt about Lori? About Josh?

3. How did Mike's displeasure affect Josh's feelings of security?

THIRTEEN

1. One of the things Josh liked best about Lori was her honesty. Why was this quality so important to him?

2. Josh asked Lori some pointed questions about her past. Did he have a right to ask such things? How do you think Lori felt when she gave him her answer?

3. What reason did Josh give for his not kissing Lori? What did he mean when he said he "so did not want to mess this thing up"?

FOURTEEN

1. Anna generally treated Josh and Mike as equals and rarely gave them orders. Why do you think she resorted

to making them serve at the soup kitchen? What did she hope to accomplish by doing so?

2. Has anyone ever disapproved of something you did or a relationship you were involved in? Were the concerns accurate? How did you handle the situation?

3. What do you think about the way Mike and Josh worked out their disagreement? Was it realistic? Can you think of a better way either could have approached this? If Anna had not intervened, what do you think would have happened?

FIFTEEN

1. Josh said he was in a "terrible spot" as his relationship with Lori grew more serious. How was it terrible? How had the events in his past colored the ways he saw himself?

2. Was Josh's response to Lori's confession appropriate? Why did he react so harshly to her confession when he had a painful secret in his own past?

3. Lori's dad had rejected her. Then Josh rejected her too. What message did she receive about her worth from these important men in her life? Was this an accurate message?

4. Josh cut Lori off swiftly and with no apparent second thoughts. How could he do this?

5. Have you ever had someone reject you? How did you react to this experience? In what ways were you able to overcome the rejection? Did you suffer any long-lasting effects?

SIXTEEN

1. How did Josh's childhood experiences affect the way he handled his breakup with Lori? What old feelings and patterns of behavior did he fall back into?

2. What old patterns do you seem to revert to when the going gets rough? How can you avoid them or choose a different path?

3. For someone who saw himself as a victim, Josh was quick to encourage Mike. Explain why he saw Mike's chances of recovery in a more positive light than he saw his own chances at a successful life. Do you think he was truly optimistic about Mike's chances or just trying to encourage himself?

4. Josh credits Mike with everything good that has happened to him. Was Mike the one responsible for the good in Josh's life? Name someone whom you believe was responsible for something positive that has happened in your life.

SEVENTEEN

1. How did Mike's illness change the dynamics of the household? How did it change Josh's role in Mike and Anna's life?

2. Mike and Anna had done many kind things for Josh. What kindness did he show to them in this chapter?

3. Josh volunteered to help Mike go to school. What did he mean when he said he wanted to do this for "for me too"?

4. Mike never asked, "Why me?" in Josh's presence. Do you think he ever thought it? Contrast Mike's attitude to Josh's general attitude about his life.

5. What elements of the blessing (see explanation on page 160) are illustrated in the scene where Mike is included in the family pictures?

6. How did Mike bless Josh when he asked him to care for Anna?

EIGHTEEN

1. How did Josh's role in Anna's life change after Mike's death? In what ways did Mike's death change Josh as a person?
2. Josh had never had anyone need and depend on him the way Anna did after Mike's death. Was Anna's dependence on Josh healthy? What do you think of her suggesting that Josh move into Mike's old room?
3. Explain Josh's curiosity about Mike's childhood.

NINETEEN

1. Was Anna surprised at Josh's discovery that she had had a daughter? Do you think she planned to tell him about Jody or to keep her life a secret? Why? Were her reasons for not telling Josh valid? What effect did this secret have on Josh?
2. Explain Josh's anger at learning about Jody. What was he angry at? Who was he angry with?
3. Why couldn't Josh accept Anna's blessing at that moment?
4. Lori told Josh that Mike and Anna had made a choice. What did she mean? What choice had they made? Do you think you could forgive or give the blessing to someone who had hurt you the way that Josh accidentally hurt Anna and later Lori? Why or why not?
5. Josh did not receive the blessing from his parents, but he did get the blessing from Mike and Anna. How did this change the direction of his life? Do you believe he and Lori were able to give the blessing to their own children?
6. Lori also had a "blessing deficiency"—she had not received the blessing from her father at a critical moment in her life. How did that affect her—especially her relationships with men? Why do you think she was able to

move past this? Did she, too, receive the blessing from someone else?

7. If you did not receive the blessing from your parents—or if the blessing was somehow incomplete—what can you do? Is this something that other people in your life have given you? Could you ask for it?

8. Who do you know that needs the blessing in their lives? Will you pass it forward and share the blessing with them or offer forgiveness?

9. Last question! Who is the first person God puts in your thoughts who could benefit from reading *A Place Called Blessing*? What would be the best way to get this person the book or encourage him or her to read it?

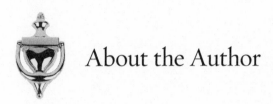

About the Author

JOHN TRENT, PHD, is president of Strong Families.com and founder of the Institute for the Blessing at Barclay College. John is a sought-after speaker and an award-winning author of more than twenty books, including six books for children. He has been a featured guest on numerous radio and television programs across the country and leads The Blessing Challenge, a joint partnership with Focus on the Family and StrongFamilies.com. John and his wife, Cindy, have been married for more than thirty years and have two grown daughters, Kari and Laura.

ANNETTE SMITH is a novelist, nurse, and a master storyteller. She has written five volumes of original short stories, two parenting books, and five novels, all set in small towns. Her fourth novel, *A Bigger Life*, was named by *Library Journal* as one of the best novels of 2007 and was a finalist in the American Christian Fiction Book Awards. Annette and her husband, Randy, have two adult children.

Join the One Million Family Blessing Challenge!

John Trent, PhD

Every child needs the blessing—the gift of unconditional love and approval that comes from one's parents. You'll see your child thrive as you learn about and give the five biblical elements of the blessing.

A Place Called Blessing is part of a trio of blessing books that launch The Blessing Campaign! Also included are the newly revised and updated edition of the best-selling parenting book *The Blessing* and the children's book, *I'd Choose You!*

These three books, along with a strategic seven-year partnership with Focus on the Family, The Institute for the Blessing at Barclay College, StrongFamilies.com, and Thomas Nelson, Inc., form the foundation for the **One Million Family Blessing Challenge**—a campaign to share the message of the blessing with a new generation of familes.

Visit www.theblessing.com and join with us to reach one million families with this life-changing message!

Available wherever books and e-books are sold

Take the Blessing Challenge today—and help your kids thrive throughout the year!

Now, Focus on the Family can support you with daily ways to live out the Blessing Challenge for years to come, no matter where you are in the parenting stages.

FocusOnTheFamily.com/parenting
> 24/7 support with content and online communities for each parenting stage.

1-800-A-FAMILY (232-6459)
> Speak with a family care specialist Monday-Friday, 6:00 a.m. - 8:00 p.m., MST.

Check out all the great resources from Focus on the Family for more ways to bless your child for years to come.

Thriving Family®
Get sensible, relevant, biblically-based marriage and parenting insights and guidance in a magazine! Each issue helps you learn more about loving your spouse, focusing on your child's age and stage, and passing on your faith to your children.

Focus on the Family® Clubhouse® and
Focus on the Family® Clubhouse Jr.®
Our monthly children's magazines give you numerous opportunities to connect with and bless your children. Hilarious jokes, activities and faith-building Bible stories can draw your family closer together . . . and closer to God.

Find these resources and more at: **FocusOnTheFamily.com/magazines.**

FOCUS ON THE FAMILY®